Collins FIELD GUIDE

WARBLER SONGS & CALLS

of Britain and Europe

GEOFF SAMPLE

First published in 2003

Collins is an imprint of HarperCollins*Publishers* Ltd.
77-85 Fulham Palace Road
London
W6 8JB

The Collins website address is:

www.collins.co.uk

09 08 07 06 05 04 03

10 9 8 7 6 5 4 3 2 1

ISBN 0 00 713974 8

Typeset by Davidson Pre-Press

Printed and bound in Great Britain by Bath Press

DIRECTORY

ACKNOWLEDGEMENTS

I'd like to thank all those who've helped me with advice and hospitality during the course of this project, including those who don't have a particular interest in birds.

Special thanks go to those who have contributed to the project directly: Marcial Yuste Blasco who helped me get the mics out into places Sennheiser never intended – and such enthusiasm; Marek Borkowski for introducing me to the magic of the Biebrza marshes and helping to make my Poland trip so rewarding; the late Pete Bull who got me out to see my first Yellow-browed and introduced me to the dubious pleasures of autumn storms on Holy Island's Snook and the Mound at Newbiggin. Linda Birch at the Alexander Library, Oxford and Richard Ranft at the National Sound Archive Wildlife Section were very kind and helpful in the use of these facilities.

I'd also like to thank the sound recordists who've allowed me to listen to and use their recordings on the CDs: Eloisa Matheu, Krister Mild, Veljo Runnel, Kyle Turner and Dave Williams. And through the National Sound Archive: H.-H.Bergmann, Seb Buckton, P.Davidson, John Gordon, P.S.Hansen, C.J.Hazevoet, Ivan Hills, Phil Hollom, Paul Holt, D.Pearson, Jean Roché, Lars Svensson and A.Wassink.

Thanks to the HarperCollins team: Myles Archibald first set me on course for the project and has been enthusiastic and supportive throughout; Katie Piper and Helen Brocklehurst have been very understanding and patient, as deadlines have passed.

Andrew Stuck, Mark Winter, Roger Boughton, Simon Elliott, Charles and Heather Myers, Michael Frankis, John Steele, Tim Cleeves, Ian Fisher, Nick Daley, Juha Paakkonen, Richard Brooks, Desmond Allen, Martin Riesing, Chris Cameron, Mike Crewe and Brian Stone have all offered help and advice in one way or another. Thanks. And others I've bumped into out and about, whose names I don't know, but were happy to share a bit of knowledge.

And lastly, though absolutely not least, many thanks to my family, Jane, Calum and Rowan, for accepting my absences and distractedness in the course of my work with good humour and unreserved support.

Despite numerous frustrations and a few low points on some of the recording trips, this project has brought me many moments when I've felt 'this is as good as it gets': a full dawn chorus on the Biebrza marshes in May; the Orpheans arriving in old almond groves on a hot Valencia hillside; the twilight singers on a still Finnish night; and quite simply all the bird song of Lesvos. And for that I'm very grateful.

INTRODUCTION

Coverage

When this guide was first discussed, the aim was to cover the regular European breeding species in reasonable depth; during the course of the work, my horizons expanded and I became interested in including firstly the autumn *Phylloscopus* vagrants, then one or two of the closely related species from adjacent regions. Soon the definition of Europe became rather fuzzy in my mind. So coverage now extends to some of the species breeding in or visiting adjacent regions, though it is usually briefer than that devoted to the widespread breeding species within the main area of Europe. Some of these are regular or occasional vagrants to Europe; others are more sedentary, but contribute to a fuller understanding of the vocalisations of their genus. I'm also hoping that this makes it a more useful guide for many travelling birders.

For all the core species, I've tried to include several examples of song and several of call, ideally from different birds. For vagrants to Europe, calls are usually more relevant, but in many cases song is included as well, for reference. This extends to some distinct races from adjacent regions where I felt it might be of interest, such as Sykes's Warbler; the examples of song and calls I heard did show differences from Booted. On the other hand the only recordings I could find of the eastern races of Lesser Whitethroat were of *blythi* calls and were arguably indistinguishable from *curruca*. This race is considered by Shirihai et al. (2001) as belonging to the same allospecies as the nominate *curruca*. So the coverage of the 'extra' species and races is a little selective, determined by the availability of recordings, information, space available in the text and CDs and budget.

The core of the work is based on my own field work, recording extensively in Britain through all seasons and in various locations on mainland Europe during the springs of the last six years. For the species covered of which I have no personal field experience, those breeding in north Africa, the islands and extremities of Europe and central Asia, my account is based on book research and on listening to recordings in the National Sound Archive (NSA), in other published sources and those of friends.

The amount of audio coverage inevitably also varies between species, depending on how much material I have myself and what recordings were available from archive and recordists' library sources.

Sources

My main literary source throughout, as will be obvious from all the references to Cramp et al., was *The Birds of the Western Palearctic* Volume VI. The copious notes on vocalisation and behaviour, while often difficult to assimilate, make this an invaluable summary of a vast amount of field observation. I've used the shorthand 'BWP' to label the numbers when referring to their categories of vocalisations under the Voice sections.

In the text I've tried to include brief notes on the social, territorial and breeding behaviour of each species, since these have such a big influence on vocal behaviour – the kinds of calls and song given, seasonal variation and male full song periods. Cramp et al. was the main source for these notes. For the same reason I've included details (where available) of where and when the recordings were made.

A major source of information and new ideas on the *Sylvia* warblers has been the recent Helm guide by Shirihai et al. (2001). Otherwise I've collated information from various sources ranging from the popular birding monthlies, such as *Birdwatch*, *Birding World* and *British Birds*, to scientific zoological journals, like *Bioacoustics* and *Animal Behaviour*. I used the *Collins Bird Guide* (Mullarney et al. 1999) to try to keep a practical focus on the material, as well as comparing notes with colleagues and other birders.

Systematics

The taxonomy and phylogeny of some of the warbler genera have been reassessed in recent years. Results of genetic analysis on various species pairs and groups have accrued at the same time as awareness of morphological detail and bioacoustic differences has progressed. The innovative proposals of Shirihai et al. regarding the phylogeny of the *Sylvia* genus make a lot of sense and I've followed their taxonomy for the genus.

Recent research by Bernd Leisler and others on species in the *Acrocephalus* and *Hippolais* genera, again incorporating mitochondrial DNA analysis, has revealed some surprising results on the relationships between species. It seems for instance that some *Hippolais* species (e.g. Olivaceous and Booted) are more closely related to the large unstreaked *Acrocephalus* warblers than to other *Hippolais* species. A reappraisal of the phylogeny of these two genera will soon, I expect, give us a clearer picture of these species and their relationships, leading to extensive taxonomic changes. Similar changes may occur in *Phylloscopus* and the other genera, to a certain extent, in time.

I think we are just at the start of a period of many changes in taxonomy and, though I've had to deal with some of the implications of the recent discoveries and proposals, it's really not my patch and beyond the scope of this work to get too involved in systematics. This is intended to be a practical reference and field guide. So I felt it best to present the species in a familiar order (more or less Voous, I think, as published by Birding World) for ease of use by the listener/reader when trying to find a species quickly.

For similar reasons I've dealt with different races and allospecies together in most cases. Particularly in the case of recent splits, it's often not clear how much the behaviour of one form is true of its relatives and past accounts may not distinguish between the two forms. Hence it seemed appropriate to discuss them together, but present the recordings of their vocalisation separately.

To make the best use of time available on the CDs, the *Phylloscopus* and *Regulus* genera have been included on the first CD with *Cettia* to *Locustella*. There are no systematic implications in this!

Labels & Terminology

Throughout the text I've used the convention of two numbers separated by a colon (e.g. 3: 10) to refer to tracks on the CDs – in this example, CD 3 and track 10, which will take you to Spectacled Warbler, beginning with song. Many of the tracks have a few different recordings, which I've numbered and referred to as S1, S2 etc. or C1, C2, representing song recordings 1 and 2 and call recordings 1 and 2 respectively. The extra track added for most species, labelled ID, has identification pointers and comparisons.

Where I've used a recording made by someone else on the CDs, I've credited the recordist in the track listings in the species accounts. Those with no recordist credited were made by myself. The times quoted are all local time, which means that the times for UK recordings from April to near the end of October are all British Summer Time (BST).

I've been using the term 'verse' for some time now in preference to 'strophe' for the individual deliveries, outbursts or instances of a species' song. Some earlier authors have used 'phrase' to refer to this (e.g. Simms 1985 and Cramp et al. 1992). Bioacoustic authors now tend to use 'phrase' for groups of sounds which form a motif within a song (e.g. Catchpole & Slater 1995): a standard Chaffinch song would usually have about four phrases under this terminology – three series of repetitions and a final flourish. I think this usage makes more sense of the term; I've probably used 'phrase' and 'motif' interchangeably, since a phrase is to speech what a motif is to music.

For the individual sounds that make up a phrase, I've used the term 'note', which bioacousticians avoid, but makes sense from a listener's perspective, along with 'syllable' or 'element'. Catchpole & Slater prefer an even more precise use of the term 'element' for any separate identifiable constituents within what we hear as an individual sound. Since this sort of detail is in the realm of the sonogram, I've used 'element' in a looser sense. In fact, as an effort to keep this a practical guide from a listener's point of view, I've avoided including or discussing sonograms at all. I think. I know too many ornithologists who are put off by them.

The difference between 'tone' and 'timbre' is a little blurred; in general usage 'tone' tends to refer to the character of purer sounds, where 'timbre' usually refers to the character of harmonic overtones in more complex acoustic sounds, typically of voices and instruments. Timbre is particularly important in dealing with bird sounds: the timbre in a species' voice is often the most constant identifying character, especially where a species has the capacity for giving a wide range of vocalisations (including possibly mimicry), which may be very similar in form to other species.

I've followed Shirihai et al. (2001) in the use of the terms 'superspecies' for groups of closely related forms showing differences to a specific level and 'allospecies' for those distinct forms. I've tried to avoid getting involved in systematics and the question of whether they are full biological species. To quote Martin Collinson from his article in *British Birds* in January 2001, 'it is concluded that the species is a real biological entity, although it is not always recognisable as such' – rather awkward for a birder in the field!

Phonetics

In bird vocalisation the basic 'lumping and splitting' dilemma – systematic categorisation – becomes particularly focused: how much do the various 'churr's and 'tsuk' of, say, Sedge Warbler represent variations on a theme or categorically different calls? What is to be gained by treating them as different calls? It certainly helps in discussing them; but maybe in terms of their use by the bird they express a continuum of changing physical and emotional states, with thresholds where some parameter of the vocalisation changes more abruptly.

Inevitably we voice the sound of a call and, when writing, spell out that sound. But our language has a limited vocabulary for talking about sound, unlike the rich source of words concerned with the visual, and sound is an ephemeral and subjective phenomenon, so over the years ornithologists have spelt out what is essentially the same call in many different ways. It would be a thankless task to try to standardise all the phonetic renditions of bird calls that have accrued. That's by way of apology for all the unpronounceable words in the text and a caution that different phonetic renderings do not necessarily refer to different calls.

I probably should apologise too for my pronunciation of the scientific names. What you get is the legacy of school Latin from thirty years ago – notably the hard 'c'. It has mostly stuck with me, but there are probably inconsistencies here and there, as I've assimilated some more contemporary anglicised pronunciation in recent years.

Recordings

I'm afraid the quality of some of the recordings is less than ideal; provided the bird's sound is reasonably clear, I've used a noisy recording when this was the only one available and I felt the subject matter warranted it. I've usually got good recordings of the commoner species, at least those common in the regions I've worked, and as you can imagine not always so good for rarer species. You get what you can to start with and try to improve from there. And the rarer vagrants don't always turn up in the most natural sounding habitats; the very obliging Hume's at Lynemouth in the winter 2001/2002 took up residence in a small plantation nestling beneath the power station, right beside the rail tracks and the lorries' entrance. But vocally it was all there.

Parabolic reflectors, as anyone who's done a bit of recording will know, are a very useful if cumbersome device for 'tuning in' to a particular sound source in a 3-D sonic environment. Rather like a telephoto lens in photography, they also act as acoustic amplifiers and raise the level of the signal – almost bring it nearer – but only across a limited frequency band. This results in a thinner but crisper sound in the recording than in real life, which is often rather useful in emphasising the detail in the complex harmonics of bird vocalisations. But it can be a little misleading as to the true nature of the sound and can detract from the real character of a bird's voice, turning it into something thinner and more strident - at worst a pain on the ears.

The only way round this is to get an 'open' mic near the subject: 'open' meaning not in a reflector. This is much more time-consuming and normally involves getting familiar with the habits of an individual subject, staking out a hidden mic on a long cable and waiting for the bird to come and do its thing on your chosen spot. By preference I use a stereo mic set-up (mid/side or ms system – if you're interested), since I like to capture something of the context and movement of my subject. I've tried to include at least one open mic recording for a species, where I've had the choice, since I feel this gives a more natural representation of the bird's voice and how you might hear it in reality.

Usually in the field I start with reflector recordings when beginning at a site or working on a new species. As I become familiar with the bird activity or the species' behaviour, I'm looking for potential subjects in good spots – situations for a reasonably close stereo recording. It's an approach that works well for me: you learn about the species and in good (quiet) locations the method provides very satisfying results.

Identification

With so many of the warbler species, it's the

combination of visuals and vocals that can be the real clincher in a confident identification. But so many are also prone to skulking in thick scrub, sedges and reeds or flitting incessantly through arboreal foliage, making it difficult to get good views. Imagine having to handle a reflector delicately and manage the recorder controls at the same time; it can be very frustrating getting a decent recording of a difficult species (suspected), but never getting that visual confirmation of identity.

This is particularly true of some of the *Locustella*, *Acrocephalus* and *Sylvia* warblers. My first experiences of the Mediterranean *Sylvia* in the south of France were like this. One evening I recorded a nice ten-minute sequence of subsong from one of these species singing in quite dense scrub; I then spent the next hour trying to get a decent look at the bird, but gave up exasperated in the growing dusk. I'm almost certain it was a Subalpine now, but the recording is obviously a bit suspect for use in what is primarily an identification guide. At many sites in the region there were Dartford, Subalpine and Sardinian Warblers in the same patches of scrub, with always the possibility of Spectacled Warbler too at some of the sites. Often there would be snatches of songs and calls all round but only occasional glimpses of birds – not easy when you're trying to learn and record their sounds.

So I've dithered repeatedly over whether to include any recordings that weren't fully visually identified.

There are some recordings where I didn't see the bird, but habitat, previous work at the location and the distinctness of the vocalisation leave no doubt in the identification. In the case of calls, with so many species having very similar calls, I've had to be very careful. It's easy to make mistakes: occasionally some other bird than your target calls unseen right in the direction of your mics.

Sometimes I find myself questioning my identification in retrospect when listening to recordings. I've got a recording of a pair of Subalpine Warblers calling in alarm, featuring a buzzing rattle behind a more stuttering one; my voice note on the tape says 'that's the male rattling'. So do Subalpine Warblers (*albistriata*) have a fast buzzing rattle or was there an Orphean or Rüppell's in the vicinity that I didn't see?

In sum, I've taken every care to ensure that the identification on the recordings is reliable; for a couple of cases where I haven't had a good visual identification or the word of a reliable companion, I've pointed the fact out in the text. But something may have slipped through the net, and if so, I'm sorry. For species of which I have no field experience or recordings, I have had to rely on others' work; but even in these cases I've tried to listen to multiple recordings and checked them against descriptions in several different field guides. Well – that's the challenge of warblers. Good luck.

CETTIA TO PRINIA

CETTI'S WARBLER *Cettia cetti*

STATUS: RESIDENT OR SHORT-DISTANCE
MIGRANT IN WESTERN AND SOUTHERN EUROPE.
SONG: EXPLOSIVE AND STACCATO; CLEAR
RINGING TONE; TYPICALLY A PAUSE AFTER
OPENING NOTES.
SONG SEASON: MOST OF THE YEAR, WITH PEAK
ACTIVITY IN THE SPRING.
CALLS: AN ABRUPT, SLIGHTLY METALLIC 'CHIT'.
CONFUSION SPECIES: NIGHTINGALE, BLACKCAP.

The only west Palearctic member of a mainly east
Asian genus, the bush warblers (Cramp et al. 1992),
Cetti's are lively birds in general behaviour and voice,
though skulking in habit. Their mating system is
sometimes monogamous, but more often polygynous;
a study in southern England found over 75% of paired
males to be polygynous, including 6 with 4 females
each (D.T.Ireland in Cramp et al.). Although the same
pair bond may persist through several years, the sexes
do not associate much. Males maintain exclusive
territories, often quite large, within which females of
polygynous males are thought to have their own
territories (Bibby in Cramp et al.). During the main
part of the breeding season, the boundaries of male
territories tend to be respected without dispute.

Male song is given throughout the year, except
during the summer moult and hard winter weather.
In breeding territories where no song has been heard
outside the breeding season, it has been assumed that
birds leave the area. Output increases in the early spring
and is at a peak during the first part of the breeding
season, with birds singing all day (Cramp et al.).

Song is in verses, though outbursts may be a more
appropriate term in the case of Cetti's, of around
2.5–5 seconds. Loud, sudden and with a clear chirping
tone, songs can be heard over 300m away in calm
conditions. Each begins with an exclamatory opening
note or two and continues after the slightest pause with
an introductory phrase leading into a repeated phrase.
Some birds have a song that splits the main section
into 2 parts (cf recording S4); none of the birds I
recorded in Greece (3 on Lesvos) had this kind of
song, though one bird did split his normal song into 2

parts on one occasion (cf recording S1).

The song is stereotyped and each male has a distinct
song-type, which he keeps for life. Each geographical
region has a basic theme and, within a region,
individuals' song-types vary in length, structure and
timbre (Cramp et al.).

Verses are delivered at long intervals while a male
patrols his territory, sometimes singing from cover and
sometimes from a prominent song-post such as the
top of a bush. Typically each verse is delivered from a
different spot; a male was noted with 24 song-posts
of which 9 were favoured (Herremans in Cramp et
al.). Normal early morning song-rate is around 1–2
verses per minute (D.T.Ireland in Cramp et al.);
2 birds I recorded in Greece and 1 in France
maintained song-rates of 3–5 per minute, just for a few
minutes around dawn. During the day the song-rate is
normally below 1 per minute. Song output is low
during incubation and nestling stages.

D.T.Ireland recorded nocturnal singing in the south
of England where males, including mated birds, sang
for long periods from a fixed song-post at very high
song-rates (max. 11.8 per minute) (Ireland 1984).
He also heard nocturnal singing from 2 first-year
males in September and October. Recording S7 was
made about half an hour before first light in Greece,
not visually identified as Cetti's, but almost certainly
this species; the continuous repetition of a song phrase
is unusual, but unfortunately I can't provide any
information as to the status of the singer or the
behavioural context.

A harsh song variant is sometimes given by the male
in alarm, accompanied by calls (D.T.Ireland in Cramp
et al.); and a harsh song has occasionally been heard
from females. Subsong is heard during the autumn
and winter, often from a male with a female nearby.

The usual contact and alarm call is a short, sharp
'chip' (BWP 2a), likened to the call of Great Spotted
Woodpecker *Dendrocopos major* but much softer. It
could easily be confused with Savi's Warbler calls;
the timbre is also slightly reminiscent of Bearded Tit
Panurus biarmicus. Since in both recordings C1 and
C2 the calls were caused by the presence of the
recordist, it might suggest that they are of BWP type
3a – a loud 'tsuk tsuk tsuk' when human intruder in

territory (De Lust in Cramp et al.). The authors go on to add 'all [these calls] may well be harder variants of call 2a'.

A metallic rattle, something like that of a Wren *Troglodytes troglodytes*, is reported for high intensity alarm. A soft 'huit' is reported as common from the female in the presence of the male and, in other contexts, a quiet squeal and a high-pitched 'peep'. A quiet, staccato 'churr' has been heard from aggressive males.

Recordings:

1: 01   Song
   1   Lesvos, Greece. 26.5.2001 6:00am. 2 sequences.
   2   Lesvos, Greece. 31.5.2001 6:30am.
   3   Lesvos, Greece. 20.5.2001 5:30am.
   4   Camargue, France. 3.6.1997 5:45am.
   6   Valencia, Spain. 19.4.2001 1:00pm.
   7   Lesvos, Greece. 28.5.2001 5:00am.
1: 02   Calls
   1   Camargue, France. 28.5.97 7:15am. Adult with young.
   2   Camargue, France. 25.5.97 8:30am. Adult (and young?).
1: 03   ID

ZITTING CISTICOLA *Cisticola juncidis*

STATUS: RESIDENT IN SOUTHERN AND WESTERN EUROPE (ALSO AFRICA AND ASIA).
SONG: SINGLE NOTE 'ZIT', REPEATED AT 1–2 SECOND INTERVALS IN UNDULATING FLIGHT.
SONG SEASON: MAINLY MARCH TO AUGUST.
CALLS: AN ABRUPT METALLIC 'PLIK'; A REPEATED 'TEW' ALSO REPORTED.
CONFUSION SPECIES: YELLOW WAGTAIL (CALLS).

Zitting Cisticolas or Fan-tailed Warblers – both accurately descriptive names – are generally rather secretive and skulking birds, not easily observed apart from the male's conspicuous song-flight and occasional scolding in the open from perched birds.

The breeding system is mostly polygynous with 50–70% of males polygynous every year. A long breeding season favours successive polygyny, with males commonly acquiring 4 and sometimes more females,

though exceptionally a male has been recorded with 5 females nesting at the same time within his territory (Cramp et al. 1992). The pair-bond is reported as weak, with little association between the sexes; territorial defence has not been noted in winter.

Male territory size has varied in different studies. It has 2 measurements: the song-flight area, which overlaps with neighbouring males over time, the actual boundaries changing from day to day, and a 'perching area', thought to be based around the nest, which is exclusive and defended (Yamagishi and Ueda in Cramp et al.).

Song is given in flight or perched and consists of a single explosive note 'zit', 'tsip' or 'dzeep', repeated at intervals of around 1 second. Song-flight is undulating, typically at a height of c.30m, and follows a roughly circular or elliptical path with a much wider range than the nesting territory; the song-notes accompany each upward swing of the undulations. The song-flight ends with a dive to ground, either into cover or to a perch, and song may continue (Guichard in Cramp et al.). Sometimes the flight swoops to near the ground and rises again. Birds I watched in Spain often ended their song-flights with excited calling.

I rarely observed perched song in Spain in April or the Camargue in May, but could have overlooked it since the song-flight is so conspicuous; it's been suggested that perched song may be locally rare or common (various observers in Cramp et al.). Males with large territories and/or many neighbours sing more in flight than perched and at a faster rate (McGregor et al. in Cramp et al.).

In the breeding season song-flights are made throughout the day. In northern France song is rare during the autumn and winter; further south in Europe it's more regular during this period, increasing in frequency from February. In Japan the main song period appears a little later than in Europe (April to September); a study here also found that aerial song duration was around 1 minute at 4:00am, peaked at c.12–13 minutes at 8:00am, declined gradually with fluctuations to 3:00pm and stopped at 7:00pm (Motai in Cramp et al.). Birds in Spain were singing quite frequently, though possibly songs of short duration, between 7:00 and 8:00pm in mid-April.

Song carries well, especially from a bird in flight; the notes are terse and high-pitched and have a sibilant, ringing quality similar to the voice of some *Motacilla* wagtail spp, but more incisive. The delivery timings are similar across all 5 birds I've recorded and each bird repeats the same note with no obvious variation, but the structure of the note varies between birds, and hence the timbre. The 2 birds in the Camargue have a similar 'song-type'; the birds in Spain included a similar type, but one bird had a rather different note, sounding more 'chüs' (recording S4). A more buzzy 'zee' is reported for Morocco, which also apparently occurs in Spain, and Cramp et al. report Chappuis' claim that unit-types occur in the Iberian and north-west African population according to geographical location.

The only call I heard regularly from the species was a sharp, metallic, quickly repeated 'plik', more abrupt and higher-pitched than Cetti's, and with a similarity to some *Locustella* calls. I heard this regularly from excited birds at the end of a song-flight (recording C2) and it sounds no different from recording C1 of a bird apparently calling in alarm (at me).

Cramp et al. describe this call (ending song-flight) as a hard 'plik', like Common Crossbill *Loxia curvirostra* flight call) and set out a schematic of various alarm, contact and excitement calls, ranging from 'zip' (BWP 2) (like song-flight) to a rapid series of 'tew' calls (3a), harsh 'zzz' calls from males (3b) and several other occasional calls. I'm not sure how the calls I recorded fit this scheme, but the authors do say it does not exclude other interpretations. Mullarney et al. (1999) give the main call as a loud 'chipp!'. Are the 'plik', 'tew' and 'chipp' different perceptions and renditions of the same call?

In recording C3 of 3 birds in a chase heading for cover, there are some other thin, buzzy *Emberiza* bunting-like calls which may well be call 3b in BWP, though said there to be from skulking males in encounters with female; I heard this several times in encounters between birds.

Recordings:

1: 04   Song
  1   Camargue, France. 25.5.1997 8:30am.
  2   Camargue, France. 4.6.1997 2:00pm.
  3   Valencia, Spain. 17.4.2001 7:00pm.
  4   Valencia, Spain. 16.4.2001 10:30am.
1: 05   Calls

  1   Valencia, Spain. 19.4.2001 7:30pm. Alarm calls.
  2   As song 4 above. Song-flight ending in calls.
  3   Valencia, Spain. 17.4.2001 7:00pm. 3 birds in chase heading into cover.
1: 06   ID

SCRUB WARBLER *Scotocerca inquieta*

STATUS: RESIDENT IN NORTH AFRICA & MIDDLE-EAST.
SONG: A BRIEF, HURRIED MELODIC MOTIF IN A CLEAR CHIRRUPY VOICE; REPEATS SONG-TYPES.
SONG SEASON: PROBABLY EARLY IN THE BREEDING SEASON.
CALLS: A DISYLLABIC WHISTLE, A SHORT TRILLING RATTLE AND A SHARP, HIGH 'CHIP'.
CONFUSION SPECIES: ZITTING CISTICOLA, GRACEFUL PRINIA.

Most accounts of behaviour are based on birds in the eastern part of Scrub Warbler's range. Pairs are mostly solitary, apart from family groups at the end of the breeding season, though some short-term association with feeding flocks of other species is noted (Potapov, Ivanov in Cramp et al. 1992). The species is apparently monogamous. Reports on shy nature are contradictory and the species may vary in this respect between geographical areas. General behaviour is said to be restless (probably the source of its specific scientific name) with wing-flicking and jerking of cocked tail, and several notes comment on mouse-like running and hopping.

Scrub Warblers are vocal throughout the year, though the central Asian races are thought to be quite different in voice from the African races (Leonovich in Cramp et al.). The recordings on the CD are from Algeria, so probably of the race *saharae*.

Male song is typically delivered fairly close to the ground, either briefly from the top of a bush or in flight (Roché in Cramp et al.). Potapov suggests that autumn pair formation reduces the need for courtship song in the spring. Nevertheless reports of song from the east of the range refer to early in the year (January and February), especially towards the end of nest-building. Birds tend to sing in the morning and evening.

Songs are a brief, sweet, melodic figure, usually descending in scale, but variable; birds tend to repeat the same form or type several times in a bout of singing. The voice and hurried melody are reminiscent of Whitethroat; songs of eastern birds include Lesser Whitethroat-like trills and whistled notes like Cetti's Warbler.

The commonest call (Cramp et al.) is a high whistle – a disyllabic 'wii-wew' (Mullarney et al. 1999); I didn't hear this on the Algerian recordings and it may be a particular call of the eastern birds. On the recordings the regular alarm call is a sharp, strident 'ship' (BWP 5b). A trilling call is said to be heard from agitated birds, and this introduces the last songs. Other calls have been noted, included a rasping rattle in alarm (Cramp et al.), though again it's not clear if this is limited to the eastern races.

Recordings:

1: 07 Song
J.C.Roché/NSA. Algeria. 25.2.1967.
Several sequences.

1: 08 Calls
As for song. Several sequences.

1: 09 ID

GRACEFUL PRINIA *Prinia gracilis*

STATUS: RESIDENT AROUND EASTERN MEDITERRANEAN, NORTH-EAST AFRICA INTO ASIA.
SONG: A REPEATED JINGLING OR GRINDING MOTIF; REMINISCENT OF *LOCUSTELLA* WARBLERS.
SONG SEASON: MUCH OF THE YEAR.
CALLS: AN ABRUPT 'CHIPP' AND A DISTINCTIVE, METALLIC TRILLING 'PRRRRR'.
CONFUSION SPECIES: SCRUB WARBLER, ZITTING CISTICOLA.

Birds are reported to maintain territory and a monogamous pair-bond throughout the year. Young birds that do not acquire a territory form nomadic flocks in autumn and winter (Paz in Cramp et al. 1992). Regarded as demonstrative birds, with various displays, and rather approachable, Graceful Prinias are considered vocal at all times of year.

The male delivers song typically from a prominent song-post (treetop, phone line or suchlike) and may move frequently between several favourite song-posts, usually on the edge of his territory. Song is also given in accompaniment to various displays and sometimes in ordinary flight.

The song period varies a little through different regions; generally it can be heard all through the year, is most intense in the first part of the year and more sporadic through autumn to winter. Paz (in Cramp et al.) found in Israel that any individual male sings for only 7–9 months and birds heard singing in July to August were mostly young juveniles. In the breeding season song can be given throughout the day, including the heat of the afternoon.

Song is in jangling or whirring verses, composed of a rapid repetition of a single syllable or motif (c.3–5 per second), with a shuffling rhythm. The performance and sound hint at the reeling of some of the *Locustella* warblers, as the singer turns his head from side to side, with wide black gape, and vibrates tail. The timbre of different individuals' songs seems to vary from metallic tinkling to a rather harsh sibilance. The main song pattern may be introduced or interrupted by call notes, and verses (or maybe 'phrases' is appropriate here) are mostly short at around 2–3 seconds, though exceptionally up to 5 minutes long, with brief intervals.

Threat at rival males includes a wing-clapping sound (recording C1), possibly produced by brushing wings and tail together (Cramp et al.); this can be delivered perched, with a jump or in flight, including a dancing display flight.

The main call used in contact and alarm (recording C1) is a short trill 'prrrr' or 'breep' (Cramp et al.), variable in voicing. Alarmed birds may give an abrupt, metallic 'chip', often in rattling series; when extended, this can sound like a section of Grasshopper Warbler song. Various ticking or zitting sounds, 'jit' and 'trrt' have also been noted (cf the end of recording C1).

Recordings:

1: 10 Song
K.Mild. Negev Desert, Israel. April 1989.
2 sequences.

1: 11 Calls
1 L.Svensson/NSA. Israel. 13.3.1993.
2 As S1.

1: 12 ID

LOCUSTELLA

PALLAS'S GRASSHOPPER WARBLER
Locustella certhiola

STATUS: SUMMER VISITOR TO CENTRAL ASIA.
VAGRANT TO EUROPE.
SONG: A RATHER *PHYLLOSCOPUS*-LIKE
REPEATED NOTE, INTERSPERSED WITH LOW
CHATTERING.
SONG SEASON: JUNE TO ?
CALLS: 'SWIT' AND A SIBILANT TICKING 'SISISISI'.
CONFUSION SPECIES: GRASSHOPPER WARBLER.

Bulkier looking birds than Grasshopper Warbler and reminiscent of Sedge Warbler particularly in the facial pattern, Pallas's Grasshopper Warblers arrive later than Lanceolated on the breeding grounds.

Males are reported to sing from low within cover, more openly higher up a bush or plant and occasionally in song-flight, and are heard mostly at night and early morning (Cramp et al. 1992).

Song is built on repeated syllables, interspersing low chattering with a louder more whistling figure, and unlike the reeling of other *Locustella* treated here. Verses are around 4 seconds long and contain a mix of repeated syllables or motifs, mostly harsh, speeding up and growing louder to a final high-pitched flourish. The final phrase is said to carry further than the rest of the verse (Svensson, Mild in Cramp et al.).

The main contact and alarm calls include a rapidly repeated, thin ticking, high-pitched and sibilant (BWP 3a), a sharp 'pwit' (BWP 3d), and a trilled, sharp 'chichurr', all just audible on recording C1. Calls heard from migrants and wintering birds are reported as similar to Lanceolated Warbler, but more rolling – 'churr' or 'cherk'; similar calls were heard from an October vagrant in northern England (Galloway in Cramp et al.). Calls were described as hard and metallic from wintering birds in south-east Asia (Lekagul et al. in Cramp et al.).

Recordings:
1: 13 Song
       K.Mild. Bratsk, Siberia. June 1987.
1: 14 Calls
       S.Buckton/NSA. Nepal. May 1990.
1: 15 ID

LANCEOLATED WARBLER
Locustella lanceolata

STATUS: SUMMER VISITOR TO EASTERN EUROPE
AND NORTHERN ASIA.
SONG: IN PASSAGES OF A PULSATING REEL;
HIGH-PITCHED, SIBILANT AND WHIRRING.
SONG SEASON: MAINLY JUNE-JULY.
CALLS: A LOW, THICK 'CHEK'.
CONFUSION SPECIES: GRASSHOPPER WARBLER,
ORTHOPTERA.

A rare breeder in eastern Europe, with autumn vagrants regularly turning up in western Europe, usually being found in coastal locations. Lanceolated Warblers are said to be very secretive and skulking, often on the ground, but reported as not particularly shy.

Song is given from a prominent perch (typically a bush at up to 6m) and from within cover. Dementiev and Gladkov (in Cramp et al. 1992) suggest that day song is usually from within cover and birds climb higher for nocturnal song, though still within the cover of foliage. Other observers have recorded different singing habits, so there may be some regional variation. Singing birds turn their heads from side to side like Grasshopper Warbler.

In Finland the most intensive singing was at night (Hario in Cramp et al.); elsewhere different singing patterns have been noted, generally with a low period in the afternoon, though said to sing all day in the far east (Kiyosu, Fujimaki in Cramp et al.).

Peak song output is in the early part of the breeding season declining to just a few birds singing in July before a slight resurgence, though some song is heard in May from early arrivals, and birds in some regions have a later song-period. Song has also been noted in wintering areas, around arrival and departure times.

Song is similar to Grasshopper Warbler, but thinner, higher-pitched and with a distinct pulse rather than the shuffle of River Warbler. The high-pitched, ringing quality is close to the stridulation of some bush-crickets (cf ID), though this may not be a problem in the breeding areas.

The main alarm and contact call is a low 'tchk', sounding like an *Acrocephalus* on all recordings at the NSA, distinct from Savi's or Grasshopper Warbler calls, but said to be variable, hard and metallic (Cramp et al.). A more prolonged, disyllabic churring call with the same timbre as the previous call is reported as an alarm call from winter birds. Lanceolated Warblers are considered fairly vocal in winter areas, but I've come across no reports of calls from vagrants to Britain.

Recordings:

1: 16   Song
      L.Svensson/NSA. Bratsk, Siberia.
      5.6.1988.
1: 17   Calls
      A.Wassink/NSA. Philippines. 6.3.1985.
1: 18   ID

GRASSHOPPER WARBLER
Locustella naevia

STATUS: SUMMER VISITOR TO CENTRAL AND PARTS OF NORTHERN EUROPE.
SONG: CONTINUOUS EVEN REEL, SLIGHTLY METALLIC AND RINGING.
SONG SEASON: APRIL TO AUGUST.
CALLS: A TERSE 'PLIK', WITH A SLIGHTLY METALLIC RING.
CONFUSION SPECIES: SAVI'S WARBLER, LANCEOLATED WARBLER, ORTHOPTERA.

While it may not be an engaging song for close listening, a singing 'Gropper' is a welcome ingredient in the soundscape of the bird's habitats and, drifting from the distance in the dusk, adds greatly to the atmosphere and character of a landscape. All the more so in Scotland and Ireland where the cooler climate doesn't allow for many bush-crickets and there's no comparable ingredient in the natural soundscape.

Although the song may be musically monotonous, it's a very efficient signal for advertising the singer's presence over a considerable area; in calm conditions it can be heard up to 300–400m away, maybe a little further on a quiet night. The level of the sound drifts as the singer turns his head from side to side; combined with sound reflections from surrounding vegetation and topographical features, this can smear the directional information in the signal – hence the so-called 'ventriloquial effect'.

Though territorial in the breeding season, there's no evidence of territorial behaviour in the wintering areas and only one record of brief song (Cramp et al. 1992). Song is heard from migrants, though of a weaker, low-intensity kind. Brief bursts of song have been heard from a female during courtship (e.g. Hoffman 1949), but this is probably rare. Birds are regularly heard still singing in August in Northumberland, England, mainly around the coastal wetlands and dune systems, but later migrants in Britain rarely sing.

The song is composed of a rapid series of pairs (c.25 per second) of elements, similar to the main call notes, the second slightly lower in pitch; the effect is essentially a mechanical trill – a fast clicking with a slight metallic ring. Verses tend to be longer at night and a continuous passage of 110 minutes was noted in Luxembourg (Cramp et al.). Verses open quietly and build to full volume over a period of a few seconds. Jingling variants to the full song, compared with Serin *Serinus serinus* and Corn Bunting *Miliaria calandra*, have been noted.

Male song is usually delivered from a low perch, about 1m from the ground, often just within the foliage or on an outstanding plant stem. Typically the bird has an upright posture, with head raised and bill wide open, and will sing from the same perch for long periods. Song can be heard at any time of the day or night, but output is highest from dusk through to mid-morning; there's evidence for variation in singing patterns in relation to latitude, with more northern birds tending to sing continuously through the summer night (Cramp et al.). Singing birds can often be observed quite closely without alarm, in one case less than 1m from an observer's face (Bell 1960); then the physical effort of producing this sound becomes apparent in the singer's vibrating body. Occasionally song is given in flight.

Calls are not heard very often. Out of many dozens of encounters with Groppers during spring and summer, including recording sessions on 9 singing males, I've only once come across bird(s) calling, but this was persistent (recording C1). The main alarm and contact call is a very short, sharp 'plik', variable to a thicker 'tchik'. This variability has caused some doubt about what constitutes a separate category of call. Comparisons have included Robin *Erithacus rubecula* 'tic' and Yellowhammer *Emberiza citrinella* 'tzit'.

Other occasional calls include a short repeated 'churr', sometimes extended in alarm, a rapid 'sisisi…', high-pitched squeaking and harsh scolding from agitated birds.

Recordings:

1: 19 Song

    1   Inverness-shire, UK. 4.6.1995 4:15am.

    2   Northumberland, UK. 17.6.1997 10:45pm.

    3   Northumberland, UK. 4.7.1999 6:30am. 2 sequences, 2nd with unusual elements.

    4   East Finland. 5.6.2002 11:00pm.

1: 20 Calls

    1   Northumberland, UK. 12.8.1999 6:30am. All sequences.

1: 21 ID

RIVER WARBLER *Locustella fluviatilis*

STATUS: SUMMER VISITOR TO EASTERN AND NORTH-EASTERN EUROPE.
SONG: A SHUFFLING CONTINUOUS REEL, WITH A WIDE BAND OF FREQUENCIES.
SONG SEASON: MAINLY MAY TO JULY.
CALLS: A SOFT, CROAKING 'CHURR' AND AN ABRUPT, WHIPLASH 'CHIK'.
CONFUSION SPECIES: SAVI'S WARBLER (CALLS); LANCEOLATED WARBLER? (SONG).

Song output is highest during the early morning and late evening at the start of the breeding season, but can be heard at any time of day or night, with some populations more nocturnal singers than others (Cramp et al. 1992). Song output generally declines during incubation and brooding, with a resumption around fledging time. Unpaired males continue to sing persistently. Song can be heard on the wintering grounds in Africa and occasionally on migration.

Birds are usually quite trusting and will continue singing if approached carefully to within 10m. They tend to have favourite song-posts, either near the top of a plant or at 2–3m in a shrub, usually in the outer foliage to the side rather than the top. If disturbed, a bird tends to head down into cover and may well start singing again at its nearest alternative song-post without having shown itself. Birds sing with an upright posture and tail slightly depressed and fanned.

Song is a daunting wedge of sound that fills a whole band of the acoustic spectrum in the riverine woodlands it occupies. The grasshopper-like shuffling rhythm is diagnostic and often compared to the sound of a sewing machine. Lanceolated Warbler song also has a shuffle or pulse, but is higher-pitched, thinner and more 'whirring' in character.

Where Grasshopper and Savi's Warbler song is a continuous trill in pairs of elements, River Warbler song is a series of sibilant pulses (c.7–15 per second), 'zi-zi-zi-zi…', producing a slightly grating timbre. On close listening very high-pitched squeaks or clicks can be heard occurring at apparently irregular intervals (probably the metallic notes reported of the Norfolk bird, June 1981).

The pulse motif (discernible by slowing down the sound or in sonograms) is reported to be constant for individuals, with probably some variation between individuals and some rare local variants.

In recording S1 it sounds as if the bird was a little nervous of the mics when he returned to his song-post: verses are short and begin with a few alarm calls, though Cramp et al. report this as characteristic of a bird changing its perch and starting a new singing session. Within a couple of minutes this bird seemed more settled and the bursts of reeling were longer. A subsequent verse from this bird was 1 minute and 45 seconds long; verses of up to 72 minutes have been noted.

It seems that the contact and alarm calls are not well known and are not heard often on the breeding grounds (Cramp et al.). They report the main contact-alarm call as a 'zick-zick', 'confusingly similar' to that of Savi's Warbler. Various other renditions are noted, including a sharp 'tschick', reminiscent of Blackcap; it's not clear to what extent these are different perceptions of the same call among various observers, different actual voicings of the call or different calls in fact. The recording from Kenya (C2) has a whiplash quality reminiscent of Spotted Crake *Porzana porzana*.

The soft, croaky 'churr' call, given sometimes as an

intro to songs, is also used for contact and alarm and may be homologous to that reported for Grasshopper Warbler. Other calls heard are quiet 'tip' calls, a noisy, high-intensity alarm call, sizzling sounds (possibly a copulation song) and a call like a short, subdued sneeze serving for nest-relief contact.

Recordings:

1: 22 Song
    1   Bialowieza, Poland. 26.5.2002 6:30am.
    2   Northumberland, UK. 19.6.1996 8:30pm.
    3   South-east Finland. 5.6.2002 1:00am. Slightly higher-pitched.
1: 23 Calls
    1   K. Turner. Hungary. May 2002.
    2   D. Pearson/NSA. Kenya. December 1988.
1: 24 ID

SAVI'S WARBLER *Locustella luscinioides*

STATUS: SUMMER VISITOR TO CENTRAL AND SOUTHERN EUROPE.
SONG: REELING, WOODEN, FASTER THAN GRASSHOPPER WARBLER, INTRODUCTORY TICKING NOTES.
SONG SEASON: APRIL TO JUNE.
CALLS: A SHARP, RATHER THICK 'PWIT'; WITH A SLIGHTLY METALLIC RING IN ALARM.
CONFUSION SPECIES: GRASSHOPPER WARBLER, ORTHOPTERA.

Song can be heard at any time of the day, but is most persistent in the morning and evening; reports vary regionally on the level of nocturnal song output, with Ukraine birds singing all night in June (Cramp et al. 1992). Peak output is at the start of the breeding season and drops appreciably on pairing, though there may be a strong resumption between broods. Song has been heard in January and more regularly from birds on spring passage and in August.

Males usually sing from near the top of a tall reed, typically one of several favourite song perches in their territories, sometimes quite close to each other. As he sings, he turns his head from side to side slowly, but with quite sudden turns, often beginning to sing a little lower, then hopping to near the top of the reed stem. The typical pose is head up, bill open wide and tail slightly depressed, showing rump. The birds I worked with sang untroubled at around 15m from me (keeping calm and quiet!), at heights of between 1–2m.

I got the impression that the general behaviour of singing males was more excitable than Grasshopper Warbler; territorial males and, to a certain extent, females are reported to show a high level of antagonism to conspecific intruders (Cramp et al.).

Verses open with a few stuttering calls, sharp ticking or crackling notes, sometimes quite prolonged as in recording S3, that accelerate and break into the more wooden-sounding reel. The introductory part does not carry as far as the main reel. Whereas Grasshopper Warbler songs also have a slightly graduated opening, building to full reel over a few seconds, the opening notes are not qualitatively different from the reel as in Savi's and this is diagnostic of Savi's. Neither Grasshopper Warbler nor Savi's has the shuffling rhythm of River or Lanceolated Warblers.

Song-bursts or verses are on average shorter than Grasshopper Warbler: average lengths for verses in various studies range from 16–35 seconds, though verses of over 10 minutes have been recorded on occasion (Cramp et al.).

Described as buzzing in Cramp et al. and a 'hard and noteless buzzing' in Mullarney et al. (1999), the reel is a stream of pairs of elements but delivered at twice the rate (c.50 per second) of Grasshopper Warbler. You can just distinguish individual pairs in Grasshopper Warbler, where Savi's blur, merging into the buzz tone. Yet Savi's is at a slightly lower pitch and lacking the metallic ring of Grasshopper Warbler.

The song has been compared with Roesel's Bush-cricket (Cramp et al.), but the pitch of this bush-cricket is much higher – an electric buzz. Several other bush-cricket species do sound very similar to Savi's though.

Described as 'not very vocal on the breeding grounds' (Gascond in Cramp et al.), birds are not heard to call very often. The main contact and alarm call is a sharp, quite loud 'pwit' (has been rendered in various ways, including 'pit' and 'tchick'); various authors suggest that there's little or no difference between this call and the introductory notes of the song. The call may be given singly, in short series or in an extended rattling series; with variations in voicing, this range of expression is presumed to signify different states of alarm or excitement in a bird.

Repeated ticking notes like the song intro accompanied by short bursts of reeling are thought to be used by the male to communicate with his mate and to act as a 'threat-song' (Cramp et al.).

Recordings:

1: 25 Song
    1 Biebrza, Poland. 23.5.2002 5:00am.
    2 Valencia, Spain. 19.4.2001 9:45am.
    3 Valencia, Spain. 16.4.2001 11:00am.

1: 26 Calls
    1 K. Turner. Hungary. May 2002.
       2 sequences.
    2 Valencia, Spain. 19.4.2001 9:30am.

1: 27 ID

ACROCEPHALUS

MOUSTACHED WARBLER
Acrocephalus melanopogon

STATUS: RESIDENT AND PARTIAL MIGRANT LOCALLY IN SOUTHERN AND EASTERN EUROPE.
SONG: A VARIED STEADY WARBLE, LIKE REED WARBLER; INTRODUCTORY SERIES OF PLAINTIVE WHISTLES.
SONG SEASON: EARLY – MAINLY FEBRUARY TO MAY.
CALLS: A SHARP 'TCHK'; A SHORT STUTTERED 'TRRRT'.
CONFUSION SPECIES: SEDGE WARBLER, REED WARBLER.

This proved to be quite an elusive species in my field work. I failed to find a singing bird on visits to the Camargue in late May and early June. The late date reduced the probability of finding a singing male and the mix of Reed Warbler song and Nightingale *Luscinia megarhynchos* song around the Capellière reserve easily misled the ear. Some birds in eastern Spain in mid-April were singing on most days, though said to be much fewer than March, the time of peak song output. It was also suggested that more songs in the early period had the diagnostic introductory section, but there are no hard data to support this.

The first bird watched sang from about mid-height from the edge of a tall reedbed (tops of the reeds c.3m). The second bird (recording S2) sang with very short breaks for over an hour in the midday sun. Several song-posts were used, all near the top of reeds in a mixed area of reedbed and open water – but not the highest stands.

Both these birds sang by open water and apparently birds tend to feed close to the water surface (Madge 1992), with the nest usually over water; though Madge also notes that birds usually sing low down and well-hidden. Taylor (1994) found on Mallorca that birds did not normally venture beyond their reedbed habitat.

The two birds I've watched and recorded and the birds on recordings I listened to in the NSA all sang in verses (or strophes) with intervals. This is at odds with some of the literature, such as Catchpole (1980) where song is described as continuous. Verses were of a variable length, usually 4–6 seconds, some shorter and quite a few longer, with the longest over 30 seconds. Simms (1985) reports song often sustained for a minute or more in the Camargue.

The character of the song is closest to Reed Warbler in the regular pace and repetitive phrasing, though a little faster and slightly higher pitched. Some of the elements hint at the grating timbre of Sedge Warbler (and occasionally the mimicry), but in all the Moustached song I've heard there's been no equivalent prolonged repetition; buzzing, grating and stuttering sequences are typically Sedge Warbler. Song has a more vigorous feel to it than the usual Reed Warbler song and this may be another reason it has been likened to Sedge Warbler (middle section of a verse).

The general impression is of a typical *Acrocephalus* warble at a steady, animated tempo in a thin voice, rather high-pitched and quite sweet on our ears.

Reports and recordings vary as to how often birds use the well-known diagnostic introductory phrasing; this is a building series of plaintive, rising whistles, usually compared with Nightingale and Woodlark *Lullula arborea*, but with a wavering quality normally lacking in similar phrases from these species. The notes gradually rise in pitch and seem to fall into two types in terms of timbre: a slightly sibilant or wheezy version and a purer whistle (cf recording ID). Simms (1985) recorded songs from birds in the Camargue with between 5 and 22 repetitions; one bird in Spain gave a 20-second sequence of 70 whistles. Simms also reports that 95% of the songs featured this introductory sequence; for the songs of the two birds worked with in Spain the figure would be well below 50%, and on some of the recordings in the NSA from birds in France there were few introductory passages.

There is a good deal of mimicry in the songs I've recorded, including the calls of Green Sandpiper *Tringa ochropus*, Redshank *T. totanus*, Great Reed Warbler (cf recording S1), Reed Warbler, Icterine Warbler, probably Melodious Warbler, though how much some of the *Acrocephaline* phrases might be a character of its own song or borrowed from some of these latter species, its close relatives, would need a more detailed study.

Some sources quote vocal observations on calls from the pair reported as breeding in Cambridgeshire in 1946 (Hinde & Thom 1947). A few questions have been raised recently about this isolated and unusual record and it seems safer now to look at other sources on voice for this species.

Vinicombe (2002) describes birds he watched in Mallorca as 'quite vocal first thing in the morning' in July. Calls were a Sedge Warbler-like 'tchik', but less hard, and a hard, grating 'ch-t-r'; the latter is probably the same call as recording C1, a little more distinctive than the thin 'tchik's I heard on recordings.

Recordings:
2: 01 Song
    1 K.Mild. Eastern Turkey. May 1990.
    2 Valencia, Spain. 19.4.2001 1:00pm.
2: 02 Calls
    1 K.Mild. Israel. December 1987.
2: 03 ID

AQUATIC WARBLER
Acrocephalus paludicola

STATUS: SUMMER VISITOR TO EASTERN EUROPE.
SONG: IN SHORT VERSES THAT ALTERNATE GRATING BUZZES WITH REPEATED WHISTLES OR 'HEE-HEE' MOTIFS.
SONG SEASON: MAINLY APRIL TO AUGUST.
CALLS: A CHURRING BUZZ, AS IN THE SONG; A LOW 'TSUK', SOMETIMES MORE EMPHATIC.
CONFUSION SPECIES: SEDGE WARBLER.

Generally skulking birds for much of the time, even singing males can be hard to see, especially in the fading evening light. The birds I listened to and recorded sang in the top layer of low sedges and other marsh plants of a very even height; those I did manage to see held an upright, stretched pose when singing. Although not particularly elaborate the song has a certain charm, especially at dusk when birds have the quiet of the meadows to themselves. On a calm evening the songs carry well and can be heard up to 300–400m away.

The mating system may be polygynous or promiscuous, with males trying to attract any available female, but maintaining no pair-bond and playing no role in incubation or rearing young. Interestingly Dyrcz is cited in Cramp et al. (1992) as noting no fighting or chasing between males in 128 hours of observation in the Biebrza marshes. Birds are said to be solitary in winter and on migration.

Song incorporates variations on a grating 'churr', interspersed with clearer voiced phrases, similar in style to Sedge Warbler, but less rambling and in short, distinct verses. With a little experience both the tone of the 'churr' and form of the motifs are diagnostic and easily separated from Sedge Warbler. Occasionally a bird will extend a verse into a more prolonged warble of 10 or more seconds, often given in song-flight. Cramp et al. suggest that some of the tonal motifs in the song are based on mimicry.

Song can be almost continuous, in verses with short intervals or with long intervals. The bird in recording S2 sang for a long period in regular verses with intervals of less than 10 seconds as dusk came on; in its final bout of singing the intervals between verses were around 30 seconds. Catchpole & Leisler (1989) found that there were 3 modes of songs: single phrases ('churr's) linked with aggressive behaviour, 2 phrases ('churr' and whistle motif) and the longest, most elaborate songs, which appeared to be more concerned with female attraction.

In various sites in the Biebrza in mid-May, the most reliable times to find birds singing were the late afternoon, around 5:00pm, and the late evening, from about 8:30 onwards. I didn't visit the marshes to check for dawn song; Cramp et al. also note a peak in song activity leading up to sunrise and a peak in song-flights between 10:00 and 11:00am.

Aquatic Warblers' calls are typical *Acrocephalus*, varying from sharp 'tsuk's, usually rather quiet and not heard often, to grating 'churr's or buzzes, indistinct from song phrases. The calls in recording C1 were not actually seen to be uttered by an Aquatic; but they were from within the area where several males were singing and quite separate from Sedge Warbler habitat.

Low 'chut' calls have been heard from migrants and song from vagrants to Britain in April (Cramp et al.). But sources suggest that, other than singing males, these are rather quiet birds.

Recordings:

2: 04   Song
    1   Biebrza, Poland. 21.5.2002 8:45pm.
    2   Biebrza, Poland. 22.5.2002 8:45pm.
2: 05   Calls
    1   Biebrza, Poland. 20.5.2002 5:30pm.
      2 sequences.
2: 06   ID

SEDGE WARBLER
Acrocephalus schoenobaenus

STATUS: SUMMER VISITOR TO CENTRAL AND NORTHERN EUROPE, EAST INTO ASIA.
SONG: BUZZING OR CHATTERING ON VARIED RHYTHMS, IN EXTENDED PASSAGES, REPEATED IMITATIONS.
SONG SEASON: MAINLY APRIL TO JULY.
CALLS: SHARP 'TSUK'S, LOW, GRATING 'CHURR'S AND SHORT BUZZES; VARIABLE.
CONFUSION SPECIES: MOUSTACHED & AQUATIC WARBLERS; REED & MARSH WARBLERS.

For us northerners the Sedge Warbler is something of a star – the only member of its genus to reach the far north of Europe and add an *Acrocephalus* voice to the marsh, riverside or lakeside communities of northern Britain and Scandinavia.

Sedge Warblers are generally vocal birds throughout the year, and conspicuously so during the breeding season. Males sing vigorously when they arrive on the breeding grounds and, although song output falls on attracting a female, continues for the rest of the breeding season at a much lower level. Birds can be heard calling during most of the nesting period and later when foraging as a family party. In August, passage birds in coastal scrub down eastern England can be heard calling at any time of day.

Birds are solitary outside the breeding season and territorial in their feeding habits. Song is sometimes heard from wintering birds, but mostly at passage times, particularly towards the spring. Males are mostly monogamous, with occasional cases of bigamy (Cramp et al. 1992). They cite one reference for female song as like a few notes of the male song.

Males sing from the top of tall marsh herbs (e.g. Cow Parsley) or low bushes like willows, often creeping to the top of the branch while singing; but they also sing from within cover. Birds often sing in low flight between song-posts and regularly make higher fluttering song-flights, rising vertically before a spiral descent.

Song is fairly unmistakable in Europe, with its buzzing or stuttering sequences of rapidly repeated elements and erratic rhythms that start hesitantly and build to intense, more complex peaks, before waning gradually. The series of staccato notes (stuttering) are distinctively Sedge Warbler in timbre – with the dry grating of the low 'churr' call or the sharp sibilance of the 'tsuk'. The shuffling rhythms are interspersed with higher-pitched whistles, generally imitations of other species, and usually repeated several times. Catchpole (1976) found that individuals' repertoires of song syllables ranged from 37 to 54; with variations in their combination, it's unlikely that any particular verse will be repeated exactly.

The song is structurally complex and although delivered in verses it's not always easy to tell where one verse ends and another begins. Catchpole found verses averaged about 20 seconds in length with a maximum of over 1 minute.

The amount of mimicry in an individual's song varies, and some birds include very little. The song can be distinguished from Reed Warbler by the erratic rhythms, pace and long series of repeated notes; overall it's also slightly higher-pitched. The long series of rather harsh, repetitive stuttering distinguishes it from Marsh Warbler.

Sedge Warbler calls show an almost continuous variation from single 'tsuk's to stuttered 'tsuk's and rattling 'churr's, all of which can be voiced soft and low or higher and more emphatically. With practise the timbre and patterns of calling become more diagnostic to the listener. They also have a rather Wren-like *Troglodytes troglodytes* spluttering call.

Recordings:

2: 07   Song
  1   Northumberland, UK. 11.5.2002 2:00pm.
  2   Eastern Finland. 6.6.2002 4:00am.
  3   Northumberland, UK. 2.5.2002 9:00am.
      Newly arrived, singing in hedge.
  4   Northumberland, UK. 15.7.1995 4:45am. Possible juvenile song – bird not seen.

2: 08   Calls
      All cuts: Northumberland, UK. May – August.

2: 09   ID

PADDYFIELD WARBLER
Acrocephalus agricola

STATUS: SUMMER VISITOR TO EASTERN EUROPE AND CENTRAL ASIA.
SONG: CONTINUOUS PASSAGES OF A BRISK, CHIRRUPY WARBLE, OFTEN LINKED WITH MIMICKED CALLS.
SONG SEASON: MAY TO JULY.
CALLS: A SHARP OR MORE SLURRED 'CHEK' AND A LOW CHURR.
CONFUSION SPECIES: MOUSTACHED & MARSH WARBLERS.

Cramp et al. (1992) found no evidence for other than monogamous breeding and, though autumn parties have been noted mixing with other *Acrocephalus*, it's said to be solitary in winter.

Males sing conspicuously from near the top of a reed, but it's not clear if the species has a special song-flight. Song has been heard in winter (Simms 1985), but is apparently given mainly in the breeding season, at a peak from May to June.

Song is in continuous passages of a musical and varied warble at a brisk pace. The voice is slightly reminiscent of Whitethroat or Garden Warbler in excited style and the fluent phrasing hints at Marsh Warbler. Passages may begin hesitantly like Marsh, but once in full flow keep a steady, swift pace, more like Garden Warbler than Marsh. The timbre has a chirruping and jingly quality ('fluently chattering' in Cramp et al.) like Serin *Serinus serinus* or Skylark *Alauda arvensis*. Several times, on recordings I listened to, a bird repeated a motif over and over, very much in the manner of some of the *Hippolais* warblers. These similarities may be more real than apparent since the species is an adept mimic and continuous passages of song may be interspersed with series of separate mimicked calls. Overall the song is slightly thin and rather high-pitched, hence the similarity to Moustached Warbler song.

Recordings of calls in the NSA included these rather *Sylvia*-like tongue-clicks (recording C1), a more Sedge Warbler-like 'tuk' and a churred call I noted as 'jjr', probably the 'cherrr' in Mullarney et al. (1999). Apparently the tongue-clicking has other voicings, ranging to a thicker or more slurred 'tschack' or 'zack' (Cramp et al.).

Recordings:

2: 10   Song
      K.Mild. Kazakhstan. June 1992.
2: 11   Calls
      P.Holt/NSA. India. 15.1.1995 11:00am.
2: 12   ID

BLYTH'S REED WARBLER
Acrocephalus dumetorum

STATUS: SUMMER VISITOR TO NORTH-EAST EUROPE.
SONG: A STEADY, UNHURRIED STREAM OF DISTINCTLY ARTICULATED NOTES AND PHRASES,

MUCH OF IT MIMICRY.

SONG SEASON: MAINLY JUNE TO JULY.

CALLS: A TONGUE-CLICKING 'TAK'; A LOW GRATING 'CHURR'; A RASPING SQUEAL.

CONFUSION SPECIES: MARSH WARBLER.

Birds I recorded in Finland sang fairly constantly between about midnight and 3:00am local time. I didn't hear any during the day, possibly because I was working afternoons and nights. I found that the song, though clear within about 40–50m and audible up to 150m, wasn't very loud; and even at 150m was easily 'obscured' by phrases from more distant Thrush Nightingales *Luscinia luscinia*. Blyth's Reed's song seemed slightly louder than Marsh Warbler or at any rate contained a higher proportion of louder phrases.

Occasionally birds would break from singing briefly, often to move a few metres to a new perch. The birds generally sang from about 2–4m in height from fairly exposed perches in bushes, occasionally coming to an outermost branch, but usually slightly within the foliage. One bird sang for a while in low vegetation within 1m of the ground. The bird in Scotland June 2000 was reported to sing for long periods during the morning but was quiet after midday (Butterfield 2000).

Koskimies (1980) found that unpaired males sing almost continuously at night; on pairing, night song ceases but shorter, subdued bursts are given during the day. The mean song period was 8 days, which all suggests that the function of song in Blyth's Reed is mainly mate attraction. He also reports that male Blyth's Reeds and Marsh Warblers were frequently found singing close together and in 1979 3 male Blyth's Reeds paired with female Marsh Warblers.

Song is a steady, unhurried series of repeated notes and phrases, clearly-articulated and mostly mimicry; often 2 motifs, one lower pitched, the other higher, are alternated. Phrases typically include *Acrocephalus* or *Sylvia* 'tak'-type notes and higher-pitched clear whistles. The delivery is much steadier than Marsh Warbler, lacking Marsh's rhythmic variation, and the phrasing much more repetitive. Overall it's a very pleasant song to listen to, fluent, with a slow, even rhythm and harmonically-rich voicings.

Although the song appears initially to be endlessly varied, repeated listening to recordings shows the same sequences of phrases and the same alternating motifs

being repeated at longer intervals. All the birds I recorded and also a recording from northern Germany included copies of Spotted Flycatcher *Muscicapa striata* alarm calls ('see-tchk, see-tchk-tchk').

I didn't hear the birds in Finland in June call much, but that might be expected early in the breeding cycle. Baker (1997) suggests that Blyth's Reed is more vocal than most of its congeners; and Harrap (1989) describes Blyth's Reed Warbler is very vociferous, giving a *Sylvia*-like 'tak' often almost constantly. The Nigg bird was said to give an occasional single loud 'tak' when skulking. An autumn bird at Portland in 2001 was reported to call a 'zeck, zeck'. This suggests birds can be quite vocal on migration stops.

The voicing of the 'tak' call varies from a thin 'tsuk' to a thicker 'tchek'. Other more distinctive calls are included in recordings C2 and C3 from wintering birds.

Recordings:

2: 13   Song
1   South-east Finland. 5.6.2002 2:15am.
2   South-east Finland. 4.6.2002 2:30am. Different bird from S1.

2: 14   Calls
1   South-east Finland. 5.6.2002 12:45am. Suspected female, not seen.
2   P.Holt/NSA. India. 5.1.1995 1:20pm.
3   P.Holt/NSA. India. 10.1.1995 2:55pm.

2: 15   ID

MARSH WARBLER *Acrocephalus palustris*

STATUS: SUMMER VISITOR TO CENTRAL AND EASTERN EUROPE.

SONG: VARIED, FULL OF MIMICRY, CHANGES PACE, BUILDS TO VERY FAST PASSAGES, LIQUID AND CHATTERING.

SONG SEASON: MAINLY MAY TO JULY, TO A LESSER DEGREE AT OTHER TIMES.

CALLS: A RATHER THICK 'CHEK'; A GRATING 'CHURR'; A RASPING SQUEAL.

CONFUSION SPECIES: REED WARBLER, BLYTH'S REED WARBLER.

Marsh Warblers spend more time in their winter areas than on their breeding grounds and are relatively late arrivals in spring. Song is reported as regular to defend loose winter territories (Cramp et al. 1992). Song is also recorded as quite frequent on spring passage. Males sing in earnest almost as soon as they arrive on the breeding grounds.

The breeding system varies between monogamy and opportunistic polygyny (Leisler in Cramp et al.) and the species is single-brooded. Most pairings are monogamous, but a small percentage of males show tendencies to try to acquire another mate or attempt to pair with neighbours' females. Mate-fidelity is said to be rather low compared to other passerines.

Males usually sing from low perches (1–2m from the ground) within cover and from prominent plant stems, sometimes a little higher, from the top of a bush or in a tree, but rarely in flight. Song output varies individually, but is generally highest at the start of the breeding season and declines on pair formation, with unpaired males continuing to sing persistently. Full song may still be given in territorial competition and subdued song for the female in courtship and nesting activity. Some neighbouring males gather for 'social singing' during the breeding season, as with Reed Warblers (Cramp et al.), and a few resume song after breeding. Juvenile song is heard in August, but otherwise birds are reported as quiet in autumn (Cramp et al.).

Song is generally most intense in the early morning, but early in the breeding season birds can sing at a high rate for much of the day and night, with a lull in the afternoon. Nocturnal song is thought to be mostly from unpaired males.

Not generally as loud as either Icterine or Sedge Warbler, Marsh's song does not carry well, probably not even to 100m when a bird is singing from cover and obscured by other species' song. Although song is more or less continuous (and categorised as such in Catchpole 1980) most of my recordings (probably all in the case of those recorded from potential breeders) show a loose verse structure. A verse passage tends to begin a little hesitantly, quickly becoming more rhythmic and sustained, building usually to a fast and furious passage mixing various motifs, before subsiding to an inconclusive end. Most, possibly all, syllables are based on accurate imitations of other species; the repertoire range is the highest of European *Acrocephalus* species.

Such a varied song is not easy to characterise, but it is marked by fast rippling liquid phrases, rhythmically varied chattering motifs (often using sparrow *Passer* or Magpie *Pica pica* phrases), 'lip-sucking' sounds and several syllables with a buzzy, nasal wheeze, similar to Icterine Warbler, but not so strident or harsh.

Walpole-Bond suggested that a nasal 'za-wee' phrase was a diagnostic phrase in every Marsh's song. Dowsett-Lemaire (1979a) suggested this was an imitation of a call of Southern Puffback *Dryoscopus cubla* and identified 13 species that were found in all the repertoires of the Marsh Warblers in the study. Others have referred to 'zee-chay' and 'ti-zaih'; I can't say for certain which is the original 'za-wee', but the ID section has examples of this kind of syllable that seem to be included in most repertoires.

The nature of the mimicry and the models for the imitations were studied in depth by Dowsett-Lemaire; around half of the repertoire of individuals was found to be based on imitations of African species. See Reed Warbler below for 'mixed-style singers' and Reed and Blyth's Reed Warblers for hybridisation (only female Marsh recorded in hybrid pairs).

The main calls are a rather thick 'chuk', sometimes a sharper 'tek' and a low, grating 'krrra' in the recordings. Several recordings at the NSA had a stuttering chatter, sounding a little like a Magpie *Pica pica*, in a voice similar to the previous calls. The recording C1 also has a nasal squeal, probably an anxiety call. Dowsett-Lemaire (1979b) gives a detailed account of Marsh Warbler vocabulary.

Recordings:

2: 16 Song
    1 Biebrza, Poland. 23.5.2002 5:30am.
    2 Northumberland, UK. 1.6.1999 5:15am.
    3 Lesvos, Greece. 20.5.2001 10:00am. Migrant, not seen well.

2: 17 Calls
    1 J.Gordon/NSA. Austria. 30.6.1977. 2 birds together in alarm.

2: 18 ID

REED WARBLER *Acrocephalus scirpaceus*

STATUS: SUMMER VISITOR TO MUCH OF
LOWLAND EUROPE, EXCEPT FAR NORTH.
SONG: CONTINUOUS PASSAGES OF A STEADY-
PACED WARBLE: CHIRRUPING, GRATING AND
SQUEAKY.
SONG SEASON: MAINLY MAY TO JULY.
CALLS: A LOW, RASPING 'CHURR'; A MUFFLED
'CHEK'.
CONFUSION SPECIES: SEDGE WARBLER, MARSH
WARBLER, EASTERN OLIVACEOUS WARBLER.

Breeding is territorial and normally monogamous, with occasional bigamy; birds are reported to defend temporary territories on autumn migration and to hold small feeding territories in winter quarters. In a study in central England roughly a third of both sexes paired with the same mate as the previous year (Catchpole in Cramp et al. 1992). Though generally skulking and often hidden in the reeds, birds are not particularly shy of humans.

Males typically sing clinging to a reed stem with head raised, sometimes low down and concealed, sometimes nearer the top of the plant, but not often in an exposed position. They have 2 or 3 favourite song-posts and several less favoured; choice for use is influenced by the singing activity of neighbours and weather conditions (Springer in Cramp et al.). Sometimes birds sing in flight, for instance in courtship, but there's not a special song-flight.

Song output is highest at the start of the breeding season; output is reduced, but does not cease, with pairing and unpaired males will continue to sing persistently. Song is at a peak in the first few hours of the day, declines to midday with a resumption in the late evening. Some unpaired males continue to sing through the night. Later in the breeding season, roughly June to August, song from paired males in colonies is concentrated in a well-synchronised dawn and evening chorus – 'social song' (Catchpole in Cramp et al.). Song is sometimes heard from autumn migrants and low intensity song from birds on winter grounds, building in strength towards spring departure.

The songs I've recorded during the breeding season in various locations in England, southern France, Spain, Greece and Poland show a surprising homogeneity; elements vary, but the pacing, rhythms of repeated phrases and overall timbre remain fairly constant throughout. Song is sometimes given in shorter bursts like verses but is usually continuous, typically a steady stream of repeated syllables (usually 2–3 times), where lower churring syllables alternate with higher, squeaky, often disyllabic ones – like Great Reed, but not so raucous, gruff and loud (their Dutch names are little and big 'karekiet'). Overall the timbre of the voice tends to be rather nasal and wheezy.

The amount of mimicry in the song varies from very little (or at least unrecognised) to a marked tendency in some birds. Singing birds may give isolated song elements between more intense and continuous bouts of song; where these are based on mimicry, they can be quite confusing. Recording S2, from a bird in Poland, features Marsh and Icterine Warbler mimicry; both species were fairly common in the vicinity.

There have been a number of Reed Warblers in Britain in recent years initially claimed as Marsh Warblers (e.g. Pagham June 1999, Kenwith Valley NR June 2000), mainly due to the amount of mimicry in the song. But both of these birds mainly sang with the steady pace and timbre characteristic of Reed; both were also suggested to be possible hybrids at some point and the Pagham bird variously a Marsh mimicking a Reed Warbler and a Reed Warbler responding to the Marsh mimicking a Reed!

Lemaire (1977) discusses a number of cases of male Reed Warblers encountered in continental Europe singing mixed Reed/Marsh song, several of which paired with female Marsh Warblers. Mixed song is described as a 'succession of rather short fragments of the song of both species directly juxtaposed'. Although the Marsh Warbler phrases were highly mimetic, with a more liquid timbre and more rapid in tempo and style of rhythms, they were slower in delivery and more nasal than normal Marsh phrasing.

Pearson et al. (2002), discussing the eastern race *fuscus*, suggest that its song is more deliberate with a slower delivery. Birds in the Göksu delta, Turkey, are reported as including a distinctive 2-note phrase in their songs, like a hand-saw (2 per second, for up to 6 seconds, descending slightly in pitch), otherwise song was as nominate. They also add that this motif is not found in the songs of *fuscus* in Kazakhstan, so may just represent regional variation.

Cramp et al. report other kinds of singing: a less continuous territorial song, a quieter conversational song and subsong, some of which may be heard from females (particularly associated with human approaching nest).

The usual contact call is a rather soft and low 'churr' (recording C1), given as a harsher variant in threat (BWP 4) and as a harsh, grating Sedge Warbler-like churr in alarm (BWP 7a) or less often a monosyllabic 'chek' (recording C3). The call at the end of recording C1 may be Reed 7a or in reality a Sedge Warbler: I wasn't able to verify. The calls in recording C2 may be the threat call or alarm call as described in Cramp et al. There was much activity in this group of Reed Warblers at the time and the call seemed to be given at other conspecifics and at me.

Other calls include a high-pitched, thin 'tsi' from the male, associated with courtship, and thrush-like or piping notes in excitement (reported in Cramp et al.).

Recordings:

2: 19   Song
    1   Suffolk, UK. 3.6.1993 5:15am.
        2 males in a 'song duel'.
    2   Biebrza, Poland. 22.5.2002 6:00pm.
    3   Lesvos, Greece. 22.5.2001 7:30am.

2: 20   Calls
    1   Biebrza, Poland. 22.5.2002 8:30am.
    2   Lesvos, Greece. 22.5.2001 8:00am.
    3   Kent, UK. 9.6.1997 6:30am.
        Identity only probable – bird not actually seen giving the call.

2: 21   ID

GREAT REED WARBLER
Acrocephalus arundinaceus

STATUS: SUMMER VISITOR TO MUCH OF EUROPE EXCEPT THE OCEANIC NORTH.
SONG: GRUFF, RAUCOUS, ALTERNATING LOW GRATING ELEMENTS WITH HIGH SQUEAKY ONES; LOUD.
SONG SEASON: MAINLY APRIL TO JULY, BUT CAN BE HEARD AT OTHER TIMES.
CALLS: LOW AND HOARSE: A SHORT, THICK 'TCHUK' AND LONGER 'CHURR'S.
CONFUSION SPECIES: OLIVE-TREE WARBLER, REED WARBLER; MARSH FROG.

Sexual relationships are complex in Great Reed Warblers. Catchpole (1983) describes the species as a partial polygynist. Bensch and Hasselquist (1992), by radio-tracking 13 females released into a new area, found that each visited a number of territories, including those of males singing short songs (see below), before selecting males that sang long songs. Four birds selected males that already had mates. The authors conclude that polygyny in this species has arisen through female choice.

Cramp et al. (1992) report that, although birds can be found together at quite high densities, they are essentially solitary in winter. Winter singing is usually from within thick scrub and is reported as regular, including full song, especially on sunny mornings. Birds are heard singing on spring passage and quiet song has been heard from a female.

Males usually deliver full song clinging to the stem at the top of a prominent reed, just visible above the level of surrounding tops. But birds also sing from lower within the reeds (as in recording S3), more so when singing less than full song. Peak song-rate is usually around dawn (recording S1), but song is heard throughout the day and occasionally at night. Birds will sing for quite lengthy periods from a single perch before moving on to another; they often continue singing in flight between perches, but not in an ostentatious song-flight. Be aware that birds are regularly heard singing away from reed beds.

Full song is in verses opening with a repeated short, low syllable, usually twice but up to 5 times, leading into repeated low grating syllables alternating with high squeaky ones, typically 'karra-karra-kee-kee...'. Verses average about 4 seconds in length, but can be extended to 10 seconds or more. The delivery is steady, rhythmic and loud, marked by the coarse grating timbre, though some of the higher-pitched syllables are delicately articulated. The repertoire of different syllables used by an individual male is normally between 10 and 20 (Catchpole 1980); the most elaborate songs are typically from polygynous males on good territories.

Catchpole (1983) found that Great Reed Warbler song fell into 2 types: short songs (averaging c.1 second with 4 syllables) and long songs (c.4 seconds with 12 syllables). Short songs are used in territorial encounters with rival males; birds were more reluctant to approach playback of short songs. Long songs, with a repertoire of loud elements added to the basic short song structure, are only given spontaneously by unpaired males, or paired males singing beyond their territory to attract another female. Long songs cease when a female has been attracted.

Calls are all characterised by the same hoarse and grating timbre heard in the lower-pitched syllables of song. Contact and alarm, not heard too often, is a subdued, monosyllabic, thick 'tchuk' ('kshack' or 'krrack' in Mullarney et al. 1999; 'chack' in Cramp et al.). Voicing does vary from the clipped one in recording C1 to the more slurred in C2. Alarm is also expressed in a low, grating 'churr'; with an agitated bird, this rises in pitch and may be delivered as a chattering series, sounding rather Magpie-like *Pica pica*. Various soft calls are given between a pair in the breeding season, particularly near the nest (Cramp et al.).

Recording C3 features a mix of short songs, alarm and aggressive or threat calls, when a second male entered the territory of an established male (the singer in recording S1). I was actually trying to record the Fire-bellied Toads.

Song of *griseldis* race is reported as lacking the guttural croaking of Great Reed nominate and Clamorous Reed, and less squeaky or scratchy than Reed, with a rich quality reminiscent of Nightingale *Luscinia megarhynchos*. The song of *orientalis* is also said to differ markedly from the nominate race, sometimes with Nightingale-like endings.

Recordings:

2: 22   Song
    1   Biebrza, Poland. 30.5.2002 4:00am.
    2   Eastern France. 23.5.1997 7:00am.
    3   Camargue, France. 25.5.1997 8:00am.

2: 23   Calls
    1   Brenne, France. 8.6.1997 7:00am.
    2   C.Carter/NSA. Botswana. 31.3.1985.
    3   Biebrza, Poland. 21.5.2002 7:30pm. Encounter between 2 males (Fire-bellied Toad).

2: 24   ID

THICK-BILLED WARBLER
Acrocephalus aedon

STATUS: SUMMER VISITOR TO SOUTH SIBERIA; VERY RARE AUTUMN VAGRANT TO EUROPE.
SONG: CONTINUOUS PASSAGES OF A STEADY WARBLE, LIKE REED WARBLER, BUT MORE VARIED.
SONG SEASON: BREEDING SEASON, SOMETIMES IN WINTER AND SPRING PASSAGE.
CALLS: A RATHER THICK 'TCHOK'.
CONFUSION SPECIES: REED WARBLER, MARSH WARBLER; GARDEN WARBLER (CALLS).

Song is heard in the winter quarters towards departure time and on migration, as well as during the breeding season (Cramp et al. 1992). In form it is most like Reed Warbler with an unhurried, regular stream of syllables and phrases, but less repetitive and with a more varied repertoire. Elsewhere it's been compared to Marsh and Icterine Warblers (e.g. Cramp et al., Mullarney et al. 1999) in respect of the vigorous delivery.

Other songs in the NSA were reminiscent variously of Reed Warbler (steady pace with 'chirrupy' and squeaky elements) and Marsh Warbler (chattering and varied). Some phrases hint at the coarse grating of Great Reed, but never so harsh. Thick-billed is noted as a mimic, so how much these similarities are part of the style of Thick-billed or whether there is mimicry involved is not clear, though I don't suppose Thick-billed and Marsh Warblers come into contact much.

The usual call is a loose 'tchok', usually repeated, sometimes hard and metallic (Cramp et al.) or, when disturbed, a more Garden Warbler-like, slurred 'shek' (BWP 2c). Repeated sharp calls may merge into a loud chattering with churring sounds (BWP 2d). A loud, harsh, quickly repeated 'cherr-cherr-tschok' has been noted (Shirihai et al. 1995).

Recordings:

2: 25   Song
    1   P.Holt/NSA. North-east China. 25.5.1996 7:15am.

2: 26   Calls
    1   P.Holt/NSA. North-east China. 16.1.1997 10:30am.

2: 27   ID

CLAMOROUS REED WARBLER
Acrocephalus stentoreus

STATUS: LOCAL RESIDENT IN THE SOUTH-EAST CORNER OF THE MEDITERRANEAN (ASIA AND AUSTRALIA).
SONG: VOICE LIKE GREAT REED; VERSES LOOSER AND REPETITIVE.
SONG SEASON: PEAKS DURING THE BREEDING SEASON.
CALLS: A DEEP HARD 'TACK', SOMETIMES IN RATTLING SERIES.
CONFUSION SPECIES: GREAT REED WARBLER.

Clamorous Reed Warblers are reported to sing both from within cover and from exposed perches (various in Cramp et al. 1992). Reports suggest that birds are very vocal on the breeding grounds, with males singing for much of the day, and song can be heard at most times of year; birds are also said to call frequently on migration and in winter. The reports come from different areas within the species' range, but it's not clear how well the observations hold good for the different races.

Song in the nominate race is vocally like Great Reed, loud, with low coarse 'tchak's and high shrill notes, but the pattern of the repetitions is more like Song Thrush *Turdus philomelos*, repeating whole phrases sometimes 3 times. The song of a bird recorded in Indonesia was more varied and rambling, though still with a hint of Great Reed in the timbre of the voice, whereas a bird in Australia sounded rather like a Thrush Nightingale *Luscinia luscinia*, though there was a similarity in the structure of the verses to those of Great Reed. Cramp et al. report descriptions that show much variation in the song across the range of the species.

The main call is a deep, hard, abrupt 'tack', often run together into a rattle, very like a Magpie *Pica pica*, but harder. Another recording at the NSA had a more churred rattle, slowing and descending at the end. Note that this recording from India is not of the nominate race. Shirihai et al. (1995) also report a rather soft 'karrk' from nominate birds.

Recordings:
2: 28 Song
    1 P.Hollom/NSA. Israel. 12.4.1980 noon.
2: 29 Calls
    1 P.Holt/NSA. Northern India. 14.1.1993.
2: 30 ID

HIPPOLAIS

EASTERN & WESTERN OLIVACEOUS WARBLERS *Hippolais pallida opaca & Hippolais pallida elaeica*

STATUS: SUMMER VISITOR TO MEDITERRANEAN EUROPE, WITH A DISJUNCT RANGE.
SONG: MEDIUM-PACED, CYCLICAL & QUITE SQUEAKY TIMBRE (ESPECIALLY EASTERN), OFTEN IN LONG VERSES.
SONG SEASON: MOST INTENSE THROUGH BREEDING SEASON, APRIL TO JULY.
CALLS: A TONGUE-CLICKING 'CHEK', MORE CHURRED IN ALARM.
CONFUSION SPECIES: REED WARBLER, BOOTED WARBLER.

My own observations and most of the references in Cramp et al. (1992) are for Eastern Olivaceous; how far the behavioural observations hold true for Western Olivaceous is open to debate.

I watched numerous birds in several localities on Lesvos in May 2000 and May 2001 and found them very active and vocal birds in the breeding season, with high song output and frequent calls of a bewildering variety. Winter birds are reported as territorial with regular song, although of lower intensity and like subsong in style; birds are also heard singing on passage, with increasing vigour towards the breeding season (Cramp et al.). Once on the breeding grounds, song is given through much of the day, even in the heat of the afternoon, with peaks at dawn and dusk.

Song is typically given in an upright posture from a favourite perch within the foliage of a bush (often tamarisk), sometimes a more conspicuous perch, with very occasional brief song-flights. Birds often sing for several minutes in the same spot, especially in the early morning, but sometimes they sing while foraging.

The style and sound of the song bears some resemblance to Reed Warbler: the tempo is medium-paced and steady and the timbre generally rather nasal and squeaky, but the rhythm is jerky, almost stuttering and the overall pitch is higher. Beyond this, the songs of the 2 races are quite different.

The songs of *elaeica* are in loose verses of 8–10 seconds, sometimes longer (Cramp et al. report almost continuous song), that open hesitantly, often with varied calls, and quickly settle into a steady, stereotyped cyclical pattern running up and down the musical scale. The patterns are about 2–2.5 seconds long and composed of a steady stream of discrete syllables, ranging from Reed Warbler-like 'churr's and 'chirrup's to 'chek'-type calls and squeaky-toy slurred whistles.

Overall the song is rather higher-pitched than Reed Warbler and gives the impression of a jerky mechanical toy. Cramp et al. report much variation in the songs of birds from around the eastern half of the *elaeica* range. It's not clear how much this represents geographical variation or different song styles from different stages of the breeding season. Svensson (2001) suggests that the regional variation has been exaggerated through misidentification.

The songs of *opaca* are roughly at the same pace and have some similarity to *elaeica* in the timbre of the voice, but are much more varied in phrasing and rhythm, more melodic and, though with a broad similarity to *Acrocephalus* song, not so close to Reed Warbler as *elaeica*. The syllables have a greater tonal variety, may include mimicry and are interspersed with rather sweet, wheezy whistles, reminiscent of some of the Mediterranean *Sylvia*; overall the song has a more wheezing character compared to the squeakiness of *elaeica*. There's some similarity to Melodious Warbler and, since their ranges overlap, confusion between the two is possible, but songs of Melodious are at a much faster, more frenetic pace. The style of *opaca* reminds me most of the excited, 'falsetto' passages of Garden Warbler song.

The main alarm and contact call of *elaeica* is a short, high-pitched 'chit', sometimes a slightly prolonged and churred 'jjt'. In alarm birds give a more nasal 'churr', something like Whitethroat calls, which may be rapidly repeated, sometimes in rhythmic motifs.

The main call of *opaca*, judging by the recordings, is a more rounded 'chek', quite *Sylvia*-like or even sparrow-like *Passer*, but, given the varied pitching and voicing of *elaeica* calls, may not be reliably distinct from the eastern birds' calls. On the recording from Morocco the bird also gives a chattering rattle in a more churred voice and a nasal 'jerr', suggesting there may be some conformity in the use of vocabulary in the 2 forms.

Recordings:

Western Olivaceous Warbler *H. pallida opaca*
2: 31   Song
        E.Matheu. Almeria, Spain. April 2002.
2: 32   Calls
        J.C.Roché/NSA. Morocco. 29.5.1967.
2: 33   ID

Eastern Olivaceous Warbler *H. pallida elaeica*
2: 34   Song
        1   Lesvos, Greece. 22.5.2001 6:15am.
        2   Lesvos, Greece. 6.5.2000 6:30am.
        3   Lesvos, Greece. 19.5.2001 8:50pm.
        4   Lesvos, Greece. 20.5.2001 8:45pm.
            2 sequences: second is subsong.
2: 35   Calls
        1   Lesvos, Greece. 20.5.2001 9:00pm.
        2   Lesvos, Greece. 19.5.2001 8:45pm.
            2 sequences.
        3   Lesvos, Greece. 5.5.2000 8:00pm.
        4   Lesvos, Greece. 22.5.2001 7:30am.
        5   Lesvos, Greece. 5.5.2000 8:00pm.
2: 36   ID

BOOTED & SYKES'S WARBLERS
Hippolais caligata caligata &
Hippolais caligata rama

STATUS: SUMMER VISITOR TO EXTREME EASTERN EUROPE INTO CENTRAL ASIA.
SONG: IN VERSES OF A FAST, VARIED CHATTERING WARBLE.
SONG SEASON: MAINLY MAY TO JULY.
CALLS: A SCRATCHY 'DJEK' (CALIGATA); AN ABRUPT 'TECK' (RAMA)
CONFUSION SPECIES: OLIVACEOUS WARBLERS; PADDYFIELD WARBLER?

Booted Warbler, Sykes's Warbler and the Olivaceous Warblers are very similar visually and, to a large extent, vocally: for a full discussion of their identification see Svensson (2001).

Reported as generally solitary and territorial in winter, the breeding system is thought to be monogamous (Cramp et al. 1992). Booted Warblers are described as skulking and secretive all year round (though autumn vagrants are said to be less so). Song has been heard in winter, but more often subdued contact calls are given. Singing becomes more intense towards spring departure, but is not usually noted from passage birds.

Males sing from a high perch within a bush or tree, sometimes in a short song-flight or horizontal flight between bushes. Output is said to be high in the early part of the breeding season with song heard all day and even at night; reports from different areas vary over whether song ceases at incubation or continues intermittently to July.

Song is a fast chattery warble in verses of 6–8 seconds, like a speeded up Eastern Olivaceous, said to be richer sounding in the nominate race than *rama* (Redman in Cramp et al.). In both the tempo is fast and the rhythm is stuttering and jerky; like Eastern Olivaceous the pitch runs up and down the scale, but more erratically. Judging from the few recordings I've heard, there's a faster chirrupy bubbling quality in *caligata* that tends to blur syllables, where in *rama* syllables and phrasing are slightly more distinct, including chaking and whistling elements.

Svensson (2001) describes *rama* song as louder (audible up to 250m), with more scratchy and hard notes, and a distinctive suggestion of Sedge Warbler song; *caligata* song, on the other hand, is much quieter and barely audible over 100m.

The main calls, given frequently by wintering birds, are said to be an abrupt 'tek' or 'tsuk' and a subdued 'chur-r' for *caligata*; reports differ as to how variable the voicing is. On the recording of *caligata* the calls have a distinct scratchy timbre, reminiscent of Stonechat *Saxicola torquata*, 'djuk'. In more extreme alarm, a repeated 'cher' and a drawn-out, rasping, Jay-like *Garrulus glandarius* call have been noted.

On other recordings of *rama* in the NSA, the calls often had a distinctive timbre, like 2 pieces of wood being hit together, an abrupt 'clak', not so pronounced on this recording.

Cade (2000) reports a Lesser Whitethroat-like 'teck' from the Sykes's trapped on Portland, quieter and less penetrating than the calls of the Eastern Olivaceous trapped the previous year (also described as a Lesser Whitethroat-like 'teck').

Recordings:
Booted Warbler *H. caligata caligata*
2: 37   Song
          K.Mild. Novosibirsk, Siberia. May 1987.
2: 38   Calls
          P.Holt/NSA. India. January 1994.
2: 39   ID

Sykes's Warbler *H. caligata rama*
2: 40   Song
          K.Mild. Kazakhstan. June 1992.
2: 41   Calls
          P.Holt/NSA. India. 2.2.1997.
2: 42   ID

ICTERINE WARBLER *Hippolais icterina*

STATUS: SUMMER VISITOR WITH A MORE EASTERN CONTINENTAL DISTRIBUTION IN EUROPE.
SONG: VARIED LOUD OUTBURSTS, REPETITIVE AND FULL OF MIMICRY; DIAGNOSTIC SLURRED WHEEZING SQUEALS.
SONG SEASON: MAINLY MAY TO JULY, BUT ALSO HEARD ON MIGRATION AND DURING WINTER.
CALLS: A VARIABLE 'CHEK', OFTEN THICK AND SPARROW-LIKE; ABRUPT RHYTHMIC MOTIF 'CHE-CHE-TWEE'.
CONFUSION SPECIES: MARSH WARBLER, MELODIOUS WARBLER.

At the start of the breeding season male Icterines sing for much of the day; with their strident voices and high song perches, the song carries well, so a male in full song is unlikely to be missed. At this time the males are active, noisy birds, though I'm reluctant to use the term 'noisy' to describe such an accomplished vocal gymnast. During parts of the day the flow of song may be broken, with outbursts of little more than a few repeated loud syllables at longer intervals; in this mode, depending on its neighbours, a bird may blend well vocally and be less noticeable. Song output is much lower after pair formation (Cramp et al. 1992).

Generally solitary outside the breeding season, wintering birds sing regularly and are thought to be territorial (Cramp et al.), as with Melodious Warbler. Icterines are rather late to arrive on their breeding grounds and leave quite soon. The mating system appears to be monogamous and there's some evidence for territories being gathered in local clusters. Song is heard regularly during spring migration and has been noted in the autumn, though autumn vagrants to Britain are mostly silent. Song has been heard at night occasionally and subsong has been heard from females.

In full song males normally sing fairly continuously from a perch for several minutes, then move on, feed a little and begin again, in a similar way to Blackcap; song-rate is highest in the early morning. The tone of voice is pretty distinctive: most phrases are in a full, but slightly shrill or nasal voice, with more articulated phrases than Melodious and several distinctive elements, including a Brambling-like *Fringilla montifringilla* nasal, drawn-out 'zweep'.

The song is variable in structure, but includes series of distinct repetitions of either a syllable or a phrase and fast warbled runs like a Marsh Warbler or a Melodious, all with an abundance of mimicry. The fast, fluid passages never quite reach the frenetic speed of Melodious; there's a less marked cyclical pattern and repeated single elements occur at will, rather than as a building intro in Melodious. Overall the pitch of Icterine's voice is also slightly lower than Melodious, with a more strident, less squeaky timbre, whereas Marsh Warbler's voice is more rounded, with softer nasal buzzes.

Mimicry has been reported to include Black Woodpecker *Dryocopus martius* and a pump-handle (Cramp et al.); all birds I heard in eastern Poland were prone to Green Sandpiper *Tringa ochropus* imitations among others.

The main calls are a variable, typically *Hippolais* 'chek' and a rhythmic motif 'che-che-twee', rising in pitch at the end - giving a cheerful impression, noted in Mullarney et al. (1999) and variously rendered including 'deteroid' (Neumann in Cramp et al.). The 'chek' call usually has the same sparrow-like *Passer* scratchiness as Melodious, when several may be run together in a short chatter, but sometimes is given a sharper, more *Sylvia*-like emphasis, 'tch'. Harsher,

more strident or chattering variations on these are given in anxiety and agitation.

The distinctive 'dideroid' type call appears to be a double 'chek' and whistle in quick succession. The rhythm of two-shorts-long is one that Icterine is fond of: it underpins many phrases in song.

Recordings:

2: 43   Song
    1   Biebrza, Poland. 31.5.2002 6:00am. Counter-singing with neighbour.
    2   Biebrza, Poland. 24.5.2002 9:00am.
2: 44   Calls
    1   Biebrza, Poland. 20.5.2002 3:00pm.
    2   Bialowieza, Poland. 25.5.2002 4:00pm.
2: 45   ID

OLIVE-TREE WARBLER
Hippolais olivetorum

STATUS: SUMMER VISITOR TO SOUTH-EAST EUROPE, MAINLY AROUND MEDITERRANEAN.
SONG: VERSES OF A STEADY-PACED WARBLE, USUALLY CYCLING PHRASES, LIKE GREAT REED IN VOICE.
SONG SEASON: MAINLY MAY AND JUNE. ALSO IN WINTER AND ON SPRING MIGRATION.
CALLS: USUALLY A DEEP, REEDY 'TCHEK', BUT VARIABLE; ALSO GIVEN IN CHATTERING MOTIFS.
CONFUSION SPECIES: GREAT REED WARBLER, EASTERN OLIVACEOUS AND UPCHER'S WARBLERS.

I worked on Olive-tree Warblers in Lesvos, Greece, in the second half of May 2001, focusing on two groups, one in the south of the island and one in the north-west, and found them generally rather secretive, though the males were often very vocal, excitable and occasionally conspicuous. They mostly sang a verse, then moved on a little way before the next, occasionally stopping for a few minutes to deliver a longer song bout from the same perch. They tended to sing from within the branch-work of small trees, sometimes taking a more prominent perch in the outer foliage. Occasionally song is given in flight between trees.

Wintering birds are reported in Cramp et al. (1992) to be territorial and sing regularly. Song and subsong are given regularly on spring passage and song has been heard on autumn passage. There appears to be a tendency to breed in neighbourhood groups, as in some other *Hippolais* species.

Full song is given in verses of about 8 seconds length, with frequent longer continuous passages (40 seconds is the longest I recorded). The intervals between verses are about 6–8 seconds in high intensity song, but when a bird is singing more casually they can be up to 40 seconds. Birds have been reported to sing at night, especially when moonlit (Cramp et al.), and they can be found singing well during the midday heat. Often these birds at the start of the breeding season gave short snatches of notes or phrases, almost under their breath, while not singing in full voice.

Overall both in song and calls Olive-tree Warbler sounds like Great Reed; the two species share a grating, slightly rough vocal timbre, but Olive-tree's voice, though quite loud, is never so strident and harsh. Both Eastern Olivaceous and Upcher's Warblers have higher-pitched songs and Upcher's has a more Icterine style.

Verses usually open with a couple of call-like notes, 'tuk, tuk', introducing a passage of a cyclical warble at a slow, steady pace, though jerky in rhythm. The elements are voiced in a mix of grating and squeaky sounds, though not in alternating phrases like Great Reed. My first 'Olive-tree' turned out to be a Great Reed singing from within a pile of brushwood (unseen) in an olive grove several hundred metres from the nearest river vegetation. Although this bird was singing in a structurally loose way, it was still marked by the alternation of high and low phrasing.

As well as the main 'tchek' call, in various voicings, I recorded a bewildering variety of chattering, churring and 'yikkering' calls. Sometimes they introduced a song verse and it wasn't always clear whether these occurred as calls or from singing males as a brief song-like outburst (along the lines of Great Reed's short songs). Birds that became nervous of me often gave the 'tchk' call, usually flying off, and occasionally a petulant chatter in the distance. Chattering calls also seemed to be used in male to male encounters.

Although imitations aren't obvious in the main passages of song, I recorded several outbursts of very accomplished mimicry (cf ID section). On numerous occasions while in the vicinity of the birds I would hear unusual phrases or outbursts that I couldn't quite identify; I came away intrigued and with a strong impression that the vocal repertoire of this species is rich and little-known.

Recordings:

2: 46   Song
1   Lesvos, Greece. 19.5.2001 7:00am.
2   Lesvos, Greece. 23.5.2001 10:30am.
3   Lesvos, Greece. 27.5.2001 8:00am. Different group from previous birds.
4   Lesvos, Greece. 23.5.2001 1:00pm. Eastern Olivaceous in background. Subsong.

2: 47   Calls
All Lesvos, Greece. May 2001.

2: 48   ID

UPCHER'S WARBLER *Hippolais languida*

STATUS: SUMMER VISITOR TO EASTERN MEDITERRANEAN & MIDDLE-EAST.
SONG: A PLEASANT, VIGOROUS WARBLE, MELODIC AND RHYTHMIC, WITH VARIED REPETITIONS.
SONG SEASON: MAINLY THE EARLY PART OF THE BREEDING SEASON.
CALLS: A RATHER COARSE 'TECK', OFTEN REPEATED, AND A LOW 'CHURR'.
CONFUSION SPECIES: EASTERN OLIVACEOUS AND ICTERINE WARBLERS.

Breeding is thought to be monogamous and territorial, with birds found singly or in pairs in winter. Birds are often found in groups on passage and there's a suggestion that breeding territories are in neighbourhood groups, as with other *Hippolais* (Cramp et al. 1992).

Males sing with an upright posture from an exposed song-post or from within cover, often changing position at the peak of a verse. A song-flight like Barred Warbler or Whitethroat has been noted. Birds are said to be not shy and rarely skulking in the breeding season and on passage.

Song output is high on the breeding grounds while establishing territories and during pair-formation, but declines on egg-laying. Subsong is heard from birds on autumn passage in some places and song becomes more frequent in late winter and on spring passage.

Song is usually in verses of around 8 seconds length, often prolonged into more continuous passages; the structure is rather meandering and repetitive, with a bright sound and melodic phrasing. In timbre of voice, character of the phrases, repetition and mimicry, Upcher's song has something of both Icterine Warbler (including slurred, nasal whistles) and Melodious Warbler (cyclical repetitions). Overall the character is lively and rhythmic, with a wide frequency range – faster and sweeter than Eastern Olivaceous.

The main contact and alarm call is an abrupt, dry 'chack', with variable voicing from low and subdued to a louder, more emphatic syllable, often repeated when excited (like Garden Warbler). In alarm, a thicker, slurred version of previous call or a dry 'churr' is given.

Recordings:
2: 49 Song
K.Mild. Israel. April 1989.
2: 50 Calls
P.S.Hansen/NSA. Turkey. 3.7.1976.
Alarm calls near nest. 2 sequences.
2: 51 ID

MELODIOUS WARBLER
Hippolais polyglotta

STATUS: SUMMER VISITOR TO SOUTH-WEST EUROPE.
SONG: IN LOUD VERSES, OFTEN PROLONGED, OF A VERY FAST WARBLE, WITH MARKED CYCLING OF MOTIFS.
SONG SEASON: MAY TO JULY AND FREQUENT IN WINTER.
CALL: SINGLE 'CHAK'S AND RATTLING CHATTER, RATHER LIKE A HOUSE SPARROW.
CONFUSION SPECIES: ICTERINE WARBLER, MARSH WARBLER, WESTERN OLIVACEOUS WARBLER.

There's some evidence that Melodious Warblers resume territoriality in their winter areas, and song is often heard (Cramp et al. 1992). The breeding system is monogamous, though bigamy has been recorded, with a tendency for pairs to form clusters or 'neighbourhood groups'. Birds are said to be rather silent on passage (Mullarney et al. 1999).

The 6 birds I've recorded in France and Spain, all sang from heights of around 3–5m at the tops of bushes or shrubs (4–7m: Ferry in Cramp et al.), often singing from the same perch for up to 10 minutes; the Icterines, in comparison, were recorded mostly at twice this height singing from the branches of trees, usually just below the leaf canopy. Melodious Warblers will also apparently sing from within cover and excited birds in a horizontal, fluttering flight between perches – the 'butterfly-flight' in Cramp et al.

They are vocal birds in spring and song can be heard all day, with peaks in the early morning and evening. Verses usually begin hesitantly repeating a mimicked call, but quickly speed up into a sustained flow of chattering, cycled runs and repeated motifs, still with much mimicry. The birds I recorded usually sang in verses of around 10–12 seconds, ranging from 6–26 seconds occasionally. The urgent, vigorous delivery of the full flow gives an impression of hot-headedness.

Song is more regular in pattern and more evenly paced than Icterine; Melodious' voice is also slightly thinner, on a par with Olivaceous, but the delivery is at a much faster pace than Olivaceous. Overall the birds in Spain sang with more fluid phrasing, reminiscent of Marsh Warbler, compared to the rather harder chattering of those in France.

The second verse of recording S1 opens with what sounds like an imitation of Icterine's 'dideroid' call; but I've heard a recording of Melodious in France with a similar motif in its alarm chattering. It's so typical of all that's difficult and yet absorbing in warbler song. Is it a case of this warbler mimicking a close relative or has it a similar motif in its own repertoire?

The usual calls are based on a thick, scratchy 'chuk', rather like a sparrow *Passer,* often uttered in pairs or as a chattering or even rattling series when excited. In alarm the chattering calls can be prolonged, almost continuous and interspersed with snatches of song. The third sequence in recording C1 appeared to be a clash between 2 birds, but I can't guarantee that the low churring is also from one of the Melodious Warblers. A brief 'hooeet' like Willow Warbler is also reported, especially in late summer (Witherby, Géroudet in Cramp et al.).

Recordings:

2: 52 Song
1 Murcia, Spain. 27.4.2001 12:30pm.
2 Eastern France. 23.5.1997 6:00am.
3 Eastern France. 23.5.1997 6:15am.

Different bird from previous sequence.

2: 53 Calls
1 Murcia, Spain. 27.4.2001 11:30am.

2: 54 ID

SYLVIA

MARMORA'S WARBLER
Sylvia [sarda] sarda

STATUS: PARTIAL SHORT-DISTANCE MIGRANT AND RESIDENT ON WEST MEDITERRANEAN ISLANDS.
SONG: VERSES OF A CHATTERY WARBLE: HIGH-PITCHED, A FEW WHISTLES, RATTLE & CHAFFINCH MIMICRY.
SONG SEASON: MAINLY DURING THE BREEDING SEASON WITH A RESUMPTION IN AUTUMN.
CALL: AN ABRUPT, SCRATCHY 'DJJT'.
CONFUSION SPECIES: DARTFORD WARBLER, BALEARIC WARBLER.

Following Shirihai et al. (2001) Balearic Warbler *Sylvia balearica*, endemic to the Balearic islands (other than Menorca), is treated as a distinct allospecies from Marmora's Warbler *Sylvia sarda*. The split is based on DNA divergence and differences in shape, plumage and vocalisation. Here we'll only deal with vocalisation: for a full account and discussion of the taxonomic implications, see this text. On the recordings supplied, differences in both song and call are evident.

Closely related to Dartford and Tristram's Warblers, Marmora's and Balearic Warblers have allopatric ranges; Marmora's is found living alongside the similar Dartford Warbler, unlike Balearic, though apparently the latter have been found together in north-east Mallorca (Shirihai et al.).

Whereas playback experiments show Marmora's and Balearic not responding to each other's song, apparently Dartford Warbler responds significantly more to playback of Balearic's song than Marmora's song (Gargallo & Prodon in Shirihai et al.).

Birds usually sing from a prominent perch, the top of a bush or even a treetop (Cramp et al. 1992), and regularly in fluttering or jerky song-flight. Song is mainly given during the breeding season, with peak output in the early part, ceases for a while in summer and has a second period in the autumn. Song is also occasionally heard in winter.

The songs of both allospecies are in typically confusable and hurried Mediterranean *Sylvia* verses. The chattering phrases in Marmora's have a thin, scratchy, rattling quality ('whirring and/or stuttering' in Shirihai et al.), rather like Eastern Subalpine or Spectacled, but overall the song is lacking in their apparent variety and has a limited frequency range. The chattering can develop into shuffling phrases, reminiscent of Lesser Whitethroat and Chaffinch *Fringilla coelebs*. But confusingly, I find the Lesser Whitethroat comparison even more marked in Balearic Warbler's song.

Marmora's song is not so marked with melodic whistles as Spectacled or Sardinian and the chattering is less harsh; Dartford in comparison has a distinct 'burr' or 'churr' to the chattering phrases. I can't hear the Wood Warbler comparison given in Cramp et al., but that may be more apparent in the field through the interaction of the song frequencies and the acoustics of the terrain.

On recording S1 the verses of Marmora's song characteristically begin with a brief opening phrase that incorporates an element like their contact call and ends in a whistle, before rushing through a shuffling warble, rather high-pitched and thin-sounding – more 'chittering' than the equivalent phrases of Dartford, which usually also include their nasal churring call-note. Dartford's verses usually include several sweet, wheezy whistles.

Many of the songs on the recording supplied end with a 'terminal flourish' phrase, which sounds to me like mimicry of Chaffinch. The phrase varies and occurs in the middle of the first verse in recording S1.

It may be a characteristic of this particular bird; but since another song ends with the imitation of a Swallow *Hirundo rustica* 'vit' call, there could be a tendency to end with a mimicked phrase or syllable.

The Marmora's Warbler which turned up on the Suffolk coast in the UK in May 2001 was reported as singing on and off.

The main call is a terse, scratchy 'djjit' (BWP 2a, described as a loud, short and rasping 'chip' by Nicholson and a brief, dry 'tsig' by Bergmann and Helb, both in Cramp et al.), not quite like any other *Sylvia* warbler, in fact rather distinct from any other warbler call – like a thin, high-pitched Stonechat *Saxicola torquata* alarm.

Recordings:

3: 01 Song
       E.Matheu. Corsica.
3: 02 Calls
       E.Matheu. Corsica.
3: 03 ID

BALEARIC WARBLER
Sylvia [sarda] balearica

STATUS: MOSTLY RESIDENT AND SEDENTARY.
SONG: IN SHORT VERSES OF A FAST WARBLE WITH A RIPPLING REPETITIVE PHRASE.
SONG SEASON: MAINLY DURING THE BREEDING SEASON WITH A RESUMPTION IN AUTUMN.
CALLS: A SPARROW-LIKE 'CHIRRA', SOUNDING SLIGHTLY DISYLLABIC.
CONFUSION SPECIES: MARMORA'S AND DARTFORD WARBLERS.

For general singing behaviour, see Marmora's Warbler.

Overall Balearic's song is slightly lower-pitched than Marmora's, with a more musical sound to my ears ('swiftly rising and falling' in Cramp et al. 1992). There's a rather liquid rippling in place of Marmora's scratchy chattering. Verses typically have an opening phrase leading into a repeated syllable, like Lesser Whitethroat's rattle, but with a more liquid, slurred sound. Analysis shows the repeated syllable to be rather complex, made up of several distinct elements (cf sonograms in Shirihai et al. 2001).

Confusion with the song of Dartford Warbler is said to be more frequent for Balearic than for Marmora's, though the areas of contact between the two are limited. Shirihai et al. emphasise the similarity between the songs of Balearic and Dartford Warbler; from the recordings supplied I feel Marmora's gives a closer general sound to Dartford, though Balearic is around the same pitch.

The usual call is not as sharp and scratchy as Marmora's, nor so drawn-out and churring as Dartford: a quite short, but rather thick and disyllabic 'chow' or 'chirra', ('tsrek' in Shirihai et al.), with a slight nasal buzz like some sparrow *Passer* calls.

There's a hint of Whitethroat, or even Dartford Warbler, in the nasal timbre, though the form is different.

Shirihai et al. also report a hard, rather dry guttural rattle in alarm like a repeated main call syllable, a drawn-out 'zerr' and a subdued continuous 'churr-churr'.

Recordings:

3: 04 Song
       E.Matheu. Mallorca. April 1997.
       2 males in song duel.
3: 05 Calls
       E.Matheu. Mallorca. April 1997.
3: 06 ID

DARTFORD WARBLER *Sylvia undata*

STATUS: RESIDENT IN SOUTH-WEST EUROPE; SOME WINTER MOVEMENT.
SONG: IN HURRIED VERSES, ALTERNATING CHATTERING AND WHISTLES; OFTEN WITH DISTINCTIVE CALL-NOTE.
SONG SEASON: PEAK MARCH TO JUNE, WITH AN AUTUMN RESUMPTION; OCCASIONAL AT OTHER TIMES.
CALLS: A DISTINCTIVE, DRAWN-OUT, NASAL 'DJURR' AND A THICK 'TJAK', OFTEN PAIRED.
CONFUSION SPECIES: SUBALPINE WARBLER, SARDINIAN WARBLER, MARMORA'S & BALEARIC WARBLERS.

The breeding system appears to be mostly monogamous; a number of cases of 2 males attending a nest are recorded in Cramp et al. (1992), including one where the second male would often return to his own territory to sing. Where birds remain sedentary, the pair-bond and territory are maintained through the winter; otherwise birds are encountered dispersing singly or in small groups. Autumn territorial activity, including song, is also reported for September and October.

I've observed and recorded Dartford warblers in southern England in May, southern France in June and eastern Spain in April. Except when singing males were perched on a low shrub, birds tended to stay within dense scrub, occasionally emerging to call at an intruder (man or bird) in the open before returning to skulk.

Song output appears to be quite sporadic in Dartford Warbler. Cramp et al. report various observers' comments: 'not a persistent singer', prefers sunny days and is 'typically very quiet in inclement weather'. Song is said to be heard more often in the morning and at dusk (Simms 1985); the bird in recording S2 (a male in Spain with a nest and eggs in his territory) sang persistently from midday through most of the afternoon, though at a much lower rate than the bird in S1 (singing at dawn). The bird also engaged in a prolonged song duel with another, where the two sang in close proximity for over 20 minutes from various points within a small area of scrubby hillside. Where one bird (presumed intruder) sang from within low scrub, the other sang conspicuously from the top of the patch, following the covert singer every time he moved to another patch of scrub.

Full song is usually delivered from the top of a gorse bush or suchlike, with occasional fluttering song-flights either to another perch or sometimes in vertical flight returning to same perch. There are numerous reports of birds singing from higher perches and one of a bird singing while foraging in tree canopy (Cramp et al.). Song is also delivered from within cover, but may be more rambling in structure.

Song is usually in brief verses of 1.5–2 seconds, marked by whistles, chattering motifs and call-like elements (distinctive). Overall the pitch is slightly lower than Spectacled or Subalpine and the chattering phrases are nearer to Sardinian Warbler, but not so harsh. It's worth noting how similar in sound and structure the songs in the recordings are, from southern England and eastern Spain.

The main contact and alarm call is a drawn-out 'djurr' similar to Whitethroat, but with a harder, more nasal timbre. Cramp et al. also report a hard 'tucc' in alarm; I haven't heard this myself, but it may be the same call that is often combined with the 'djurr' (as in recordings C1 and C2). Like many *Sylvia*, particularly this group of the Mediterranean species, a soft 'trrt' is used for contact between paired birds.

Recordings:

3: 07 Song
1. D.Williams. New Forest, UK. June 4:00am.
2. Valencia, Spain. 22.4.2001 2pm.

3: 08 Calls
1. New Forest, UK. 27.5.1993 5:30am. Adults with young.
2. Languedoc, France. 5.6.1997 4:15pm.
3. Murcia, Spain. 27.4.2001 9:00pm.
4. Valencia, Spain. 22.4.2001 11:00am.
5. Languedoc, France. 5.6.1997 3:45pm. Juveniles.

3: 09 ID

SPECTACLED WARBLER
Sylvia conspicillata

STATUS: RESIDENT AND SHORT-DISTANCE MIGRANT IN SOUTH-WEST EUROPE AND EASTERN MEDITERRANEAN.

SONG: SHORT VERSES (USUALLY) OF A MELODIC WARBLE MIXING SLURRED WHISTLES AND CHATTERING.

SONG SEASON: MAINLY FEBRUARY, OR EARLIER IN THE SOUTH, TO JUNE; ALSO HEARD IN AUTUMN.

CALLS: IN BURSTS OF A RATHER LOUD, EVEN RATTLING, SOMETIMES STUTTERING A LITTLE; LOW 'CHURR'S.

CONFUSION SPECIES: SARDINIAN, SUBALPINE AND DARTFORD WARBLERS; WHITETHROAT.

Where resident, birds have been noted in pairs in winter, often on their territories, though small groups also have been reported outside the breeding season. The breeding system appears to be monogamous (Cramp et al. 1992).

I watched and recorded Spectacled Warblers in the Camargue, France, in May 1997 and in Valencia, Spain, April 2001; in both areas several different birds were recorded. Singing males were mostly on scrub (gorse and salicornia) within 1 metre of the ground; one bird sang occasionally from a tamarisk at over 2 metres. Scolding birds would call briefly in the open before returning to within scrub.

Song is usually in brief, hurried verses that are a series of slurred whistles at different pitches, linked by chattering sounds: tuneful, with an overall jaunty air. The whistled notes and chattering may roughly alternate; or the whistles and tonal elements can dominate and the song sounds very sweet and rambling; overall it's higher-pitched than the songs of its sympatric related species. The chattering phrases have a softer burr than most of the other Mediterranean *Sylvia*, reminiscent of Whitethroat and not as harsh as Dartford Warbler. Perched song is interspersed with song-flights on which the bird rises silently, then sings on a slow fluttering descent.

I recorded a surprising amount of variation in the singing of even the same males; Cramp et al. describe song as 'rather varied both within and between individuals'. They also report subsong as a soft faint echo of full song; there appears to be a continuum of variation between such very soft subsong and verses of full song. The 3 sequences of recording S3 were taken from a male over a period of around 20 minutes; before the last sequence, he appeared, or rather disappeared, with a second bird, presumed mate. Low intensity singing, of the more melodic subsong type, has been reported from birds in the autumn (Cramp et al.).

The most frequently heard call is a rather distinctive, fast rattle, scratchy or slightly grating, usually delivered fairly evenly, though sometimes a little stuttered, generally in bursts of a second or less.

Calls also include a softer, short 'churr', with something of a Whitethroat sound or even Dartford Warbler; and in alarm, or possibly short-distance contact, a low, soft 'trrt' similar to that of related species. Cramp et al. report a high-pitched 'tseet' as a common contact call, especially between mates (cf recording S3, second sequence).

Recordings:

3: 10 Song
   1   Valencia, Spain. 26.4.2001 7:30am.
   2   Camargue, France. 4.6.1997 5:45am. (Greater Flamingo).
   3   Valencia, Spain. 26.4.2001 10:30am. Different bird from S1; 3 sequences.

3: 11 Calls
   1   Camargue, France. 25.5.1997 2:00pm. 2 sequences. Pair near probable nest.
   2   Valencia, Spain. 25.4.2001 8:15pm.

3: 12 ID

SUBALPINE WARBLERS
Sylvia cantillans cantillans &
Sylvia cantillans albistriata

STATUS: SUMMER VISITOR TO SOUTHERN EUROPE, AROUND THE MEDITERRANEAN AND THROUGH SPAIN.
SONG: A FAST CHATTERING WARBLE, WITH SOME SWEET WHISTLED NOTES, USUALLY IN VERSES; RATHER SQUEAKY.
SONG SEASON: MAINLY APRIL TO JUNE, BUT HEARD AT OTHER TIMES (ESPECIALLY SUBSONG).
CALLS: A HARD, RATHER THICK 'TEK' (*CANTILLANS*); A HIGHER-PITCHED 'JIT', OFTEN RATTLED (*ALBISTRIATA*).
CONFUSION SPECIES: SARDINIAN, SPECTACLED AND DARTFORD WARBLERS; WHITETHROAT.

Shirihai et al. (2001) discuss the taxonomic status of Subalpine Warblers, recognising 4 subspecies of which they suggest 3 differ sufficiently to approach allospecies status. I observed and recorded Subalpine Warblers in 3 different areas: east-central Spain, southern France and Lesvos, Greece. The recordings are from these areas, covering the western (*S. c. cantillans*) and eastern (*S. c. albistriata*) races; birds were assumed to be of local races and were not visually identified beyond species.

Encountered singly, in pairs or in small groups in winter and on passage, Subalpine Warblers are territorial in their breeding, which appears to be monogamous (Cramp et al. 1992). They are generally lively and vocal birds, though they were rather elusive in southern France in early June. They can be skulking in the dense scrub of their habitats, but singing males are quite approachable – more so, in my experience, than Sardinian Warblers.

My impression while working on Subalpine Warblers was that there was wide variation in their calls and, within their broader style, songs. I was slightly sceptical of suggestions that vocalisations were categorically different between the races. On working through my recordings, however, consistent differences emerged and I've presented the recordings from the western and eastern areas separately.

Song can be heard at any time of the day and in the breeding season song output is high. Birds sing from the top of a bush or small tree, and also from within low scrub. Excited birds frequently launch into a fluttering song-flight. Song is occasionally heard during winter and subsong from birds on passage (Cramp et al.), as well as during the breeding season.

The songs I recorded (6 sessions of at least 4 different birds in western areas, 6 sessions with 6 different individuals on Lesvos) show considerable structural and tonal variation. Nevertheless full song is usually in short hurried verses of about 3 seconds, sometimes extended to 2 or 3 times this length. The warble is a mix of swift chattering phrases, tonally similar to calls and much less harsh and noisy than Sardinian Warbler, interspersed with clearer-toned elements like whistles. There's a tendency to open verses with a slightly wheezy, slurred whistle, shared with Spectacled Warbler, but Subalpine's are thinner and higher-pitched. Song has been described as similar to that of Whitethroat (Cramp et al.), but where in Whitethroat full song phrases tend to descend in pitch through a verse, verses of Subalpine tend to remain at a constant pitch (though the elements show wide frequency variation).

The songs of western birds are slightly lower-pitched and fuller-voiced than eastern birds and the whistled notes less wheezy; the rhythm of the phrasing is rather jerky, whereas the eastern birds' phrases tend to merge into a steady stream.

The main call of birds in Spain was a tongue-clicking 'chütt' or 'tek' (Shirihai et al.), rather like Whinchat *Saxicola rubetra* calls; sometimes these may be run into a stuttering series (cf background in recording C2). Contact between paired birds was a soft creaky 'trrt' (recording C3).

The main call of birds in Lesvos was a higher-pitched, thinner 'chit', often in stuttered pairs 'tret' (recording C1 first 4 sequences). More alarmed birds run the calls together into a rattle. There's some suggestion from my notes that the males call in a thinner, higher-pitched voice than the females. I haven't heard the rolling 'trrr' of the western Mediterranean islands race *moltonii*, so cannot say how distinct it is from the rattling alarm calls of the Lesvos birds, but it appears that rattling calls may not be restricted to *moltonii* Subalpines.

The eastern male singing in recording S1 was a close neighbour of the Rüppell's Warbler in recording S1 of that species; their main song-posts were about 35m apart in a rocky hollow of a scrubby hillside (near a dead goat pit, hence the flies!).

Recordings:

Western Subalpine *S. c. cantillans*

3: 13   Song
    1   Valencia, Spain. 15.4.2001 12:30pm.
    2   Provence, France. 30.5.1997 9:00am.
    3   As S1

3: 14   Calls
    1   Valencia, Spain. 22.4.2001 6:00pm.
    2   Valencia, Spain. 23.4.2001 8:00am.
    3   Valencia, Spain. 23.4.2001 7:30am.

3: 15   ID

Eastern Subalpine *S. c. albistriata*

3: 16   Song
    1   Lesvos, Greece. 7.5.2000 10:30am.
    2   Lesvos, Greece. 24.5.2001 8:30am.
    3   Lesvos, Greece. 31.5.2001 5:45am.

3: 17   Calls
    1   All Lesvos, Greece. May 2000 & 2001.

3: 18   ID

TRISTRAM'S WARBLER *Sylvia deserticola*

STATUS: RESIDENT IN NORTH-WEST AFRICA; SOME WINTER MOVEMENT.

SONG: A SWIFT CHATTERING WARBLE WITH WHISTLES.

SONG SEASON: HEARD BETWEEN JANUARY AND MAY.

CALLS: A TONGUE-CLICKING 'TREK'; SPARROW-
LIKE CHATTERING AND 'CHURR'S.
CONFUSION SPECIES: SPECTACLED AND
SUBALPINE WARBLERS.

Reports vary as to the breeding season between
Moroccan and Algerian populations: pairing is
thought to be much earlier in Morocco, but has not
been well studied (Cramp et al. 1992).

Males sing from a low but conspicuous perch, such
as the top of a bush, and sometimes in song-flight.
Song has been heard from early in the year (January
and February) on wintering grounds through to May
on breeding grounds. Output is said to be highest from
daybreak through the morning (Cuzin in Cramp et
al.). Only calls were heard in one report from late
November (Smith in Cramp et al.).

Song is in verses averaging around 3 seconds of a
very Subalpine-like warble, including rattling,
chattering and wheezy whistles. Shirihai et al. (2001)
draw attention to the clear grating tone, recalling
Dartford Warbler, as distinct from Subalpine.

The main contact and alarm call is a sharp 'tsuk'
(like Blackcap) or a more disyllabic 'trek' or 'chirr-it'
(like House Sparrow *Passer domesticus*), sometimes
also given in a rattling or stuttering series. A 'tscherr'
or 'zerr' has been noted from males in chases (Koenig
1895 in Cramp et al.).

Recordings:
3: 19   Song
    1   J.C.Roché/NSA. Morocco. 16.3.1966.
    2   J.C.Roché/NSA. Algeria. 18.2.1967.
3: 20   Calls
    1   As for song. 2 sequences, from
       Morocco and Algeria respectively.
3: 21   ID

SARDINIAN WARBLER
Sylvia melanocephala

STATUS: RESIDENT AND PARTIAL MIGRANT IN
SOUTHERN EUROPE AROUND THE
MEDITERRANEAN.
SONG: IN VERSES OF A FAST WARBLE, MIXING
CALL-LIKE CHATTERING WITH SWEET WHISTLES.
SONG SEASON: MAINLY FEBRUARY TO JUNE, BUT

ALSO HEARD IN THE AUTUMN.
CALLS: SOMETIMES A SINGLE 'TSUK', MORE
OFTEN IN STUTTERING OR RATTLING SERIES;
RHYTHMIC MOTIFS.
CONFUSION SPECIES: SUBALPINE, DARTFORD
AND RÜPPELL'S WARBLERS.

Reports suggest that territories are often established
in the autumn and occupied through the winter in
many areas, when birds tend to be encountered singly
or in pairs. The breeding system appears to be
monogamous (Cramp et al. 1992). Notes on the song-
period vary, with song said to be heard throughout the
year in some areas (e.g. Malta), but there appears to be
a general lull from late summer through the autumn.

My observations and recordings come from three
areas: east-central Spain, the south of France and
Lesvos in Greece. I found Sardinian Warblers
generally rather skulking and secretive, but not slow to
come forward and deliver what sounds like a stream of
abuse at anyone walking in the vicinity – a
characteristic sound of the Mediterranean maquis, as
harsh as the dry, thorny scrub the bird inhabits.

I've found them to be a little shy in singing. Not only
were there often few males singing, but they tended to
switch to the alarm calls and rattles when approached
to within about 50m. On the other hand the bird in
recording S3 eventually ended up singing from the top
of a bush c.6m from me in full view. Lovely – thank
you, that bird.

Song is usually delivered with an upright and alert
posture from a prominent perch at the top of a bush
and frequently in a fluttering song-flight, either
vertically with a return to the same perch or moving on
to another song-post. But I've also heard birds
continue singing, usually a more subsong-like warble,
when they've entered low scrub.

Full song of the male is in fast verses (average length
c.3 seconds) of a rattling warble incorporating slurred
whistles. The rattling is hard-edged in timbre and, as in
the calls, diagnostic; the whistles may be full and clear
or have a wheezy, sibilant timbre. Verses almost always
open with a whistle. Occasionally singing birds will slip
into a more prolonged warble, often with sweeter
whistles and squeaks (recording S3), as in the song-
flight. Overall Sardinian song gives a surprisingly
melodic impression for a bird with such harsh calls; it's

also normally rather louder and fuller than Dartford, Spectacled and Subalpine Warbler song. A song bout often ends with a few calls.

Birds call frequently and easily break into alarm calls. Usually calling is in a stuttering, chattering or rattling series of hard 'tuk' or 'tr' notes, often compared to Wren *Troglodytes troglodytes*, but sometimes heard as single syllables. Different regions appear to have distinct call motifs used by the birds for contact between neighbours and almost as a song substitute outside the breeding season (Cramp et al.). When alarmed, birds tend to run the calls into a continuous series, which may rise in pitch to almost a screech when agitated. Other calls include a softer, more churred 'trrt' and a soft, slightly squeaky 'kuk' (like a distant Water Rail *Rallus aquaticus*), probably for contact within a family group.

Recordings:

3: 22   Song
    1   Lesvos, Greece. 19.5.2001 6:30am.
    2   Murcia, Spain. 27.4.2001 7:15am.
    3   Valencia, Spain. 26.4.2001 12:30pm.
    4   Provence, France. 2.6.1997 9:00am.
3: 23   Calls
    1   Lesvos, Greece. 5.5.2000 9:00am.
    2   Provence, France. 2.6.1997. Several
       sequences.
    3   Valencia, Spain. 18.4.2001 &
       20.4.2001. Several sequences.
3: 24   ID

RÜPPELL'S WARBLER *Sylvia rueppelli*

STATUS: SUMMER VISITOR TO SOUTH-EAST EUROPE, MAINLY AROUND MEDITERRANEAN.
SONG: IN SHORT FAST VERSES OF A SHUFFLING CHATTER (LIKE LESSER WHITETHROAT), WITH BRIEF WHISTLES.
SONG SEASON: MAINLY MARCH TO JUNE, BUT HEARD OCCASIONALLY AT OTHER TIMES.
CALLS: A SLIGHTLY SIBILANT, EXPLOSIVE 'PWIK', OFTEN RATTLED (BUZZY).
CONFUSION SPECIES: SARDINIAN WARBLER, SUBALPINE WARBLER; SWALLOW, ROCK NUTHATCH (CALLS).

Song has been heard from wintering and migrant birds, including a vagrant on the Shetlands in the autumn, and there are reports of aggressive males on spring migration in chases uttering chattering calls and subsong (Cramp et al. 1992); otherwise there is little information on territoriality outside the breeding season. Breeding appears to be monogamous.

I observed and recorded a number of individuals in May 2000 and May 2001 in two separate localities on Lesvos, Greece. The behaviour of singing males was broadly similar to Sardinian, but the habitat more arid and rocky. Song-posts were usually outstanding branches in the top of lower scrub, though small trees and rocks are cited in Cramp et al. I found birds much less prone to call in the breeding season than closely related species; in about 6 hours observation of the song area of different males' territories, only 3 short sequences of loud calls were heard.

Although I heard song at dawn, all my recordings were made once the sun had warmed up the morning; in the case of recording S1, the bird sang almost constantly over a 2-hour period in the midday heat. Bouts of singing were regularly interspersed with song-flights to other song-posts.

Song is in verses normally of 1.5–5 seconds, characterised by a fast, shuffling chatter, not as harsh as Sardinian Warbler, nor so thin and chittery as Subalpine. Tonal syllables tend to be brief and rather squeaky and may be imitations of other species. The recordings suggest mimicry of sparrow *Passer* species, Goldfinch *Carduelis carduelis*, Blackbird *Turdus merula* and possibly Bee-eater *Merops apiaster*.

The basic call syllable has a hint of *Locustella* timbre and sounds rather like Swallow's *Hirundo rustica* 'vit' call, but can have a thicker voicing (ID); in alarm these break into a rattle, sounding thinner and buzzier than the individual syllables, with something of a bubbling quality. The calls in recording C1 were from a probable female in the territory of the male singing in S3. I also heard soft 'trrt' calls, with a similar timbre to the other main calls, from an adult male joining a female or juvenile.

Recordings:

3: 25   Song
    1   Lesvos, Greece. 7.5.2000 11:00am.
    2   Lesvos, Greece. 25.5.2001 10:30am.

3   Lesvos, Greece. 30.5.2001 8:30am.
3: 26 Calls
    1   Lesvos, Greece. 29.5.2001 8:00am.
         2 sequences.
    2   Lesvos, Greece. 7.5.2000 10:00am.
3: 27 ID

ASIAN DESERT WARBLER
Sylvia [nana] nana

STATUS: MIGRATORY IN MIDDLE-EAST DESERT;
(MAINLY RESIDENT IN NORTH AFRICA.)
SONG: SHORT VERSES OF A SIMPLE TUNE, IN A
CLEAR VOICE, INTRODUCED BY A CHURRED 'KRRR'.
SONG SEASON: MAINLY MARCH TO JUNE (SEE
BELOW).
CALLS: A FAST, SHARP 'JI-JI-JI...' AND A RATTLING
'KRRRR'.
CONFUSION SPECIES: WHITETHROAT, DESERT
LESSER WHITETHROAT.

The two allopatric forms of Desert Warbler are
considered by Shirihai et al. (2001) to differ enough in
plumage and vocalisation to be treated as a
superspecies consisting of Asian Desert Warbler
S. [nana] nana and African Desert Warbler
S. [nana] deserti, the latter less studied.

Breeding is territorial and appears to be
monogamous. Outside the breeding season birds tend
to be met with singly or in pairs, though small parties
have been encountered in Volga-Ural sands in
September (Cramp et al. 1992). Though skulking in
habit, birds aren't considered shy (especially vagrants
to England) and are vocal all year round.

Males sing from the top of a bush or within cover
and sometimes on the ground; some birds make
parachuting song-flights between song-posts. Song is
at a peak from spring to early summer and can be
heard from sunrise to a little after sunset with a lull in
the afternoon. African birds are known to sing in the
winter months from December, building to full song
from March to April; Asian birds sing from arrival on
the breeding grounds in April to June mainly, though
there's a record of song in August (Cramp et al.).

The songs of the 2 allospecies are rather different.
That of the African *deserti* is in short verses (average
c.1.5 seconds) at lengthy intervals, of a Whitethroat-

like warble, with an introductory descending 'krrr',
sometimes omitted, and a final rising whistle. The song
of *nana* has a similar overall structure, but the main
section is a stereotyped tune in a clear, slightly
chirrupy voice. Subsong has been heard in winter
months and during breeding.

The main contact and alarm calls are thought to be
similar in both forms (Shirihai et al.): the purring 'krrr'
first syllable of the song (lighter in *nana*), a quickly
repeated strident syllable 'ji-ji-ji' suggesting Blue Tit
Parus caeruleus, but variously rendered, and a chattering
rattle. This last call may just be a more emphatic and
prolonged version of the purring 'krrr'. A 'wee-churr',
sounding like Grey Partridge *Perdix perdix* has also been
noted (various in Cramp et al.).

Recordings:
3: 28 Song
       K.Mild. Kazakhstan. June 1992.
3: 29 Calls
       K.Mild. United Arab Emirates. Jan 1999.
3: 30 ID

MÉNÉTRIES'S WARBLER *Sylvia mystacea*

STATUS: SUMMER VISITOR TO THE EXTREME
SOUTH-EAST OF EUROPE AND MIDDLE-EAST.
SONG: SHORT, UNHURRIED, MELODIC VERSES,
MIXING CLEAR AND SCRATCHY SYLLABLES.
SONG SEASON: MAINLY APRIL TO JUNE.
CALLS: AN ABRUPT 'TCHK', OFTEN GIVEN IN
STUTTERING OR RATTLING SERIES.
CONFUSION SPECIES: EASTERN ORPHEAN
WARBLER, SARDINIAN WARBLER.

Birds have been noted singly and in pairs in winter
and in small parties in late winter and spring. Breeding
appears to be monogamous, but the social habits and
breeding behaviour of Ménétries's Warbler are not
very well known (Cramp et al. 1992). General
behaviour is restless and wary, like Sardinian Warbler.

Males sing from an exposed perch on a bush,
frequently changing song-posts, and often in a
fluttering song-flight. Song is heard on spring
migration, peaks from April to June on the breeding
grounds and is sometimes heard a little later. Subsong
has been heard from males in winter.

Song is in verses of variable length, often with only brief intervals; the pattern is a steady, varied warble mixing harsher chattering with clear-toned syllables. It's usually said to be like Sardinian Warbler song, but slower and with a more jerky rhythm (Mullarney et al. 1999) and 'more musical, with diagnostic harsh and loud tongue-clicking notes' (Shirihai et al. 2001). Also described as conversational and rather quiet. Judging by recordings at the NSA, the song has something of the quality of Eastern Orphean, with rich, almost Nightingale-like *Luscinia megarhynchos* phrases, lacking the frequent rattling phrases of Sardinian. I don't know whether this is influenced by mimicry.

Calls include a short 'tchk', usually run together in series; more commonly reported (and on NSA recordings), are various harsh rattling 'trrr's and 'trr-tr-tr', but described as softer than Sardinian (Hollom et al. in Cramp et al.) and closer to Rüppell's (Shirihai et al.). Again judging by the recordings, Ménétries's call syllables sound harder, though less 'noisy' than these species, and when rattled remind me as much of Barred Warbler as of Sardinian.

Recordings:

3: 31   Song
         L.Svensson/NSA. South-central Turkey.
         22.5.1989.
3: 32   Calls
         L.Svensson/NSA. South-central Turkey.
         May 1989.
3: 33   ID

CYPRUS WARBLER *Sylvia melanothorax*

STATUS: RESIDENT AND SUMMER VISITOR TO CYPRUS.
SONG: VERSES OF A CHIRRUPY WARBLE, STEADY-PACED THOUGH RATHER JERKY IN RHYTHM.
SONG SEASON: MOST INTENSE MARCH TO JUNE, BUT HEARD ALL YEAR EXCEPT JULY TO SEPTEMBER.
CALLS: A SHARP 'CHEK' AND A SCRATCHY 'ZRIK'; A HIGH-PITCHED FAST TICKING AND A LOWER RATTLE.
CONFUSION SPECIES: SARDINIAN & RÜPPELL'S WARBLERS.

There's evidence (including prolonged song period) for territorial defence all year round, both from Cyprus and from other winter areas, though small groups are seen together at passage times. The breeding system is thought to be monogamous (Cramp et al. 1992) and, aside from territorial males, birds are said to be generally shy and skulking.

Males sing in an upright pose with raised crown feathers from favoured, conspicuous song-posts and sometimes in a butterfly-like song-flight. At the start of the breeding season birds often sing throughout the day, with a lull in mid-afternoon.

Song is in verses, averaging around 3 seconds in length, of a fast chattery warble like Sardinian Warbler, but with a more wooden timbre (Bergmann and Helb in Cramp et al.) or chirping burr, in place of Sardinian's harsher stuttering. This chirruping quality, reminiscent of House Martin *Delichon urbica*, is considered diagnostic by Shirihai et al. (2001). It also differs from Sardinian song in the relative lack of whistled notes. Subsong rich in mimicry is said to be given early in the breeding season.

The usual contact and alarm call is a sharp, percussive 'chek', sometimes a more rasping 'zrik' from males (recording C1), which may be associated with flight. In alarm a high-pitched, ticking rattle has been recorded and, from aroused birds, lower churring rattles (recording C1), reminiscent of Spectacled Warbler. Mullarney et al. (1999) also note a hoarse, drawn-out 'tschreh tschreh ...' from agitated birds.

Recordings:

3: 34   Song
         J.Gordon/NSA. Cyprus. 27.5.1985.
3: 35   Calls
         H.-H.Bergmann/NSA. Cyprus.
         30.3.1978. From male bird.
3: 36   ID

WESTERN & EASTERN ORPHEAN WARBLERS *Sylvia [hortensis] hortensis & Sylvia [hortensis] crassirostris*

STATUS: SUMMER VISITOR TO SOUTHERN EUROPE (MEDITERRANEAN).
SONG: VERSES OF A MUSICAL WARBLE IN A RICH, BURRED VOICE; REPETITIVE IN HORTENSIS,

FASTER AND MORE VARIED IN CRASSIROSTRIS.

SONG SEASON: MAINLY MAY TO JULY, OCCASIONALLY EARLIER.

CALLS: A BLACKCAP-LIKE 'TACK' AND A SLIGHTLY HISSY RATTLE, STUTTERING OR CONTINUOUS.

CONFUSION SPECIES: THRUSH SPP.; BLACKCAP, GARDEN WARBLER.

Shirihai et al. (2001) treat Orphean Warbler as a superspecies comprising the two allopatric populations, which DNA studies have shown to be 'surprisingly divergent genetically'. Visually the differences between these two allospecies are slight and song is considered the only reliable field character for identification between the two.

More than any other of the warbler species I've worked on, the Orpheans fired my musical imagination. Both allospecies sing in a rich, fruity voice and though the Western's song is rather repetitive, I was lucky enough to catch the males just setting up territories in Spain and often singing more varied patterns than usual. The Easterns have had me laughing to myself at the sheer verve of their songs. So the common name is well-chosen in its reference to the mythical master musician.

Birds are often found in small groups in the winter quarters and song appears to be rare in winter (Cramp et al. 1992). Pairing seems to be monogamous; territories are considered to be quite large for a *Sylvia* warbler and song-posts may be up to 200m from the nest site. Several times on Lesvos early in May I came across groups of four, and possibly five birds, including two males and two females, moving slowly but quite actively and vocally low through scrub – behaviour that puzzled me.

The pitch and timbre of the voice is similar through both forms but verse composition differs: western birds normally have a short verse with an introduction and a repeated motif; eastern birds' verses have more varied phrasing and use a wider range of motifs.

WESTERN ORPHEAN *S. [h.] hortensis*

The singing males I observed in Spain tended to sing from within the dense cover of small trees, at the Valencia site usually Holly Oaks. The birds were skulking, but fairly approachable when singing.

The high incidence of subsong, more varied verses than usual and several chases (with snatches of subsong) suggested that pairing was taking place; but I didn't actually see much of the birds and never identified a female, so it is also possible the chases were between males just setting up territory. A male encountered in southern France in June was singing in full voice, while foraging through low, scattered scrub, stopping every 10–12 seconds to deliver a verse.

When not slipping into subsong or delivering a few more excited verses, the verses of the western males tended to be quite brief and the gaps between them rather long, often 10 to 15 seconds for periods of several minutes during the day. Verses have a brief opening leading into a repeated motif, the syllables of which include 'chak's, 'churr's and thrush-like *Turdus* whistles. The burr in timbre is like Garden Warbler or Mistle Thrush *Turdus viscivorus*. With a more distant bird the phrases can be reminiscent of Blackbird *T. merula* or Song Thrush *T. philomelos*. The birds in Spain in April, as well as typical quiet subsong (recording S3), also occasionally sang more varied verses (recording S2) similar in form to Eastern Orphean songs, but always returned to more repetitive verses after a while.

I only heard a few rather soft 'tack's from these birds; sources note no difference between the calls of eastern and western birds. Further calls are provided for Eastern Orphean.

Recordings:

3: 37　Song

　　1　Valencia, Spain. 25.4.2001 2:00pm. 3 sequences (2nd with intervals shortened).

　　2　Valencia, Spain. 24.4.2001 4:00pm. Varied song.

　　3　Valencia, Spain. 25.4.2001 1:30pm. Subsong: probably different bird from S1.

3: 38　Calls

　　Valencia, Spain. April 2001.

3: 39　ID

EASTERN ORPHEAN S. [h.] crassirostris

For me this is musically the most entertaining songbird in Europe. The relatively low pitch brings it closer to our hearing's main coverage; birds sing loudly and are fairly trusting, though don't like to be approached too close.

Males were singing well in May on Lesvos. Often birds would sing casually while foraging, but even these would stop at some point to deliver a series of verses from a single perch, usually in the outer branches of the top half of a small tree, an olive or an oak. One bird was singing as it moved through a high pine canopy. The only song I observed on the wing was in level flight between perches, but Cramp et al. report a more ostentatious song-flight rising to 10–12m between perches.

Song was most frequently heard on mornings once the sun had warmed things up, but Cramp et al. report peak singing early in the morning and late afternoon to dusk. In Tunisia song is reported to be heard throughout the day in June. It appears that song output and its diurnal rhythms are at least variable and may be sporadic.

The song has often been compared to Nightingale *Luscinia megarhynchos* in guides, but is more varied in both rhythm and phrasing. Like western birds *crassirostris* song has thrush-like *Turdus* phrasings and a slight rolling or bubbling timbre to the voice. Tonally, whistles and flutey elements, subtle scratchy sounds and reedy 'churr's are all mixed together in hurried phrases that include trills and brief repetitions. The tempo is fast, with sudden changes of rhythm.

There is mimicry (e.g. the first verse of recording S3 has a Swallow *Hirundo rustica* imitation) but it doesn't appear to play a large part in song normally.

The usual calls are a typical *Sylvia* sharp 'tchak', lower-pitched and slightly fuller than most of its congeners; this call is run into a rattle in alarm, with the voicing varying from a harsh, stuttering chatter to a more rolling churr, broadly similar to Barred, Rüppell's and maybe even Sardinian Warblers. Several times I came across females giving a sort of strained squeal call, repeated for long periods, usually moving low through open scrub, but in one instance from the same spot for over 15 minutes.

Recordings:

3: 40 Song
    1   Lesvos, Greece. 26.5.2001. 7.30am. Casual song; intervals edited.
    2   Lesvos, Greece. 11.5.2000 8:30am.
    3   Lesvos, Greece. 19.5.2001 8:00am.

3: 41 Calls
    1   All recordings from Lesvos, Greece. 22–27.5.2001.

3: 42 ID

ARABIAN WARBLER *Sylvia leucomelaena*

STATUS: RESIDENT AROUND THE RED SEA
SONG: A FULL, FLUTEY, MUSICAL WARBLE IN SHORT VERSES.
SONG SEASON: ALL YEAR ROUND; PROBABLY MOST INTENSE FEBRUARY TO APRIL.
CALLS: A RATHER THICK, LOW 'CHAK' AND A HARD RATTLE.
CONFUSION SPECIES: ORPHEAN WARBLERS, UPCHER'S WARBLER, BLACKBIRD.

It's likely that pairs maintain their territory through the year; birds are seen singly or in pairs through the winter months. The mating system is monogamous, with mates forming a close pair-bond (Cramp et al. 1992).

Males sing from a conspicuous perch high in a tree and possibly in an occasional song-flight. Song is reported as almost throughout the year (Shirihai in Cramp et al.); other reports suggest February to April is the period of highest output. Song has been heard to start in poor light before sunrise and it's likely that there's a lull in song during the afternoon heat. Females have been heard singing and subsong has been heard in November.

Song is in short verses of a loud, sprightly, musical warble, including call-like and guttural elements and fluted notes, with a quality compared to thrush *Turdus* species and Eastern Orphean Warbler, though not so fast and varied. The pattern is considered rather stereotyped and repetitive (Cramp et al., Shirihai et al. 2001). The songs in the recordings probably exaggerate the variation since they are not all consecutive; songs 2 to 4 of recording S1 do appear to be consecutive and show motifs repeated in subsequent verses, with a small variation each time.

Calls heard on recordings at the NSA include a soft, quite thick 'chack', reminiscent of Great Reed Warbler in timbre (recording C1), a repeated hard 'jik' from a female near nest and young, sometimes rapidly repeated with a pebble-hit sound, an Orphean-like rattling 'trrrr' (recording C2) and a nasal, wheezy 'jwee', probably the juvenile call 'zwii' in Shirihai et al.

Recordings:

3: 43   Song
    1   P.Davidson/NSA.Yemen. 1993.
3: 44   Calls
    1   P.Hollom/NSA. Israel. 29.4.1979.
       4:50am.
    2   P.Davidson/NSA.Yemen. 1993.
3: 45   ID

BARRED WARBLER *Sylvia nisoria*

STATUS: SUMMER VISITOR TO EASTERN EUROPE AND CENTRAL ASIA.
SONG: VERY LIKE GARDEN WARBLER, BUT MORE REPETITIVE, SLOWER-PACED AND IN SHORTER VERSES.
SONG SEASON: MAY TO JUNE.
CALLS: A THICK 'CHAK', COARSE RATTLES AND A RASPING 'TCHEW'.
CONFUSION SPECIES: GARDEN WARBLER.

Barred Warblers are vocal birds with a complex repertoire in the breeding season, but fairly silent at other times (Cramp et al. 1992). Whereas some populations are thought to breed monogamously, one study revealed that over 4 years 50-75% of males attempted to gain a second mate. Pairs are often found in neighbourhood groups.

Song can be heard at any time of day, but output is reported as highest at dawn, later on sunny mornings and towards dusk (Cramp et al.), though I didn't hear much song in the evening in Poland. Song has been heard on moonlit nights in Tajikistan and noted from wintering birds in Africa leading up to spring passage.

The males I watched in Poland in May all sang from quite prominent perches, usually the top of a bush or small tree, either within the edge foliage or more conspicuously, and sometimes at the top of a patch of lower scrub; they usually had at least three favourite perches. Singers often held a rather horizontal pose, with their head forward, throat feathers ruffled, and tail lowered and spread. Song-flights between song-posts were quite frequent. They were rather excitable and aggressive birds (at least the males), but this behaviour may be confined to early in the breeding season, since the species is considered one of the most skulking of *Sylvia* outside the male display period (Cramp et al.).

Song-flights often rise jerkily to 10–15m, returning to the same or a nearby song-post, feature slowed wing-beats, rather than fluttering, and may include an audible wing-clapping (recording S3).

The song voice has a fruity burr similar to Garden or Orphean Warbler, though described as harsher than Garden Warbler (Cramp et al.) and harder and more rasping (Mullarney et al. 1999). Delivery of full song is in short verses at a steady pace with brief gaps; phrases juxtapose higher-pitched and lower-pitched elements to give the song a melodic, sing-song quality to our ears. The abundance of rich, slurred brief whistles creates an overall liquid impression.

Though the actual composition of each verse varies, there is a strong theme of repetition, with one or two phrases often running through a series of verses. As a rule, it's easier to discern melodic phrases in Barred Warbler song, helped by the tendency for repetition, where Garden Warbler song is so constantly hurried and varied that phrases become blurred; likewise the verses of Barred sound more tightly structured than the apparent rambling of Garden Warbler.

Excited or disturbed birds often give the rattling call leading into or mixed with the song. The impression that this is common may be influenced by birds being set on edge by the presence of the observer. Birds I observed singing for a period undisturbed and unchallenged didn't mix the rattling call with the song.

The main calls include a thick 'tchak', not especially loud, but usually repeated; and a fairly distinctive coarse rattle. The rattle is sometimes given in a more stuttering delivery, reminiscent of Sardinian Warbler.

The rasping 'tchew's on recordings C1 and C2 seems to be the call referred to in Shirihai et al. (2001) as a buzzing 'dajj', in Cramp et al. as 'dziu' or 'drau' and maybe the hoarse, muffled 'chaihr' in Mullarney et al. According to Cramp et al., this call (and also a sharp 'chuff' in a similar voice) is only frequent at the start of the breeding season, associated with territory establishment and pair formation, and described as a male-to-male challenge-call. The timbre is similar to shrike *Lanius* calls, which is intriguing, given the association with Red-backed Shrike *L. collurio* on breeding territories.

Recordings:

3: 46   Song
    1   Biebrza, Poland. 21.5.2002 9:00am.
    2   Bialowieza, Poland. 26.5.2002
        11:30am.
    3   K.Turner. Hungary. May 2002.
3: 47   Calls
    1   K.Turner. Hungary. May 2002.
    2   Biebrza, Poland. 28.5.2002 2:30pm.
3: 48   ID

LESSER WHITETHROAT *Sylvia curruca*

STATUS: SUMMER VISITOR TO MUCH OF EUROPE, EXCEPT THE WEST, AND INTO CENTRAL ASIA.
SONG: IN BRIEF VERSES WITH A SHORT SOFT WARBLE INTRODUCING A WOODEN RATTLE.
SONG SEASON: MAINLY APRIL TO JULY, OCCASIONAL OTHERWISE.
CALLS: A SHARP 'TEK' USUALLY; ALSO NASAL RATTLES AND 'CHURR'S AND A VERY HIGH-PITCHED 'SEE'.
CONFUSION SPECIES: BONELLI'S AND ARCTIC WARBLERS, CIRL BUNTING, YELLOWHAMMER; BLACKCAP (CALLS).

The species is considered monogamous and male song has been found to peak during the pre-fertile period, then decline abruptly (Klit 1999). Most males did not sing when their mate was fertile. Cramp et al. (1992) report a case where a paired male resumed song 4 days after his young fledged. Subsong can be persistent at the start and end of the breeding season and is heard during migration and in winter. The male of an isolated breeding pair in Lancashire, UK, in 1998 was heard to sing from 2nd May to 10th, but not after. Breeding was confirmed when 2 birds were seen carrying food to young in June (C.Davies personal communication.).

Song is usually given by birds moving within cover, changing position then stopping to deliver the next verse; sometimes birds sing from a high perch in a tree. Cramp et al. report song as occasional in flight, usually horizontal but with fluttering wing-beats. Peak of song output is in the early morning, but song can be heard all through the day and has been heard before daylight in Syria and from a disturbed bird at night.

The male's song is in 2 parts: a rather Whitethroat-like fast warble and a quickly-repeated Chaffinch-like *Fringilla coelebs* syllable forming a rattle, or 'twitter and trill' respectively in Klit. In normal territorial singing the warble serves as a brief introduction to the rattle, or may be dropped altogether. A listener further than 30m from a singing bird may not hear the introductory warble at all, but the rattling part carries well.

Sometimes some very high-pitched, whistled 'see' notes (BWP 3) are heard between verses or given separately from song (e.g. recordings S1 and C2). The sound is considered unique to the species. The rattle is formed from syllables made up of 2 elements, so is a true trill, sounding rather like Bonelli's Warbler song or even a short Cirl Bunting *Emberiza cirlus* song.

The study by Klit suggested that the 2 forms of song were adapted for communication over different distances. The twitter form, more prevalent early in the breeding season and important in male-female interaction, is a shorter distance signal; the trill form, dominant later and associated with male-male territoriality, is a long distance signal. On the other hand the study also found that individuals repeatedly used twitter during quarrels when 2 males were close (cf recording C2 with 2 males excited over a female). Whereas the twitter form was found to be variable (warbled), the trill was stereotyped in length and composition: 14 males had 1 type of trill, 1 male had 2 types.

The tongue-clicking 'tek' call has a slightly more sibilant or hissy timbre than other similar *Sylvia* calls, in fact more a lip-sucking 'tsuk'; but it's probably only readily distinguishable in the field from Blackcap's similar call with attuned ears. Recordings C1 and C2 show that Lesser Whitethroats have quite a vocabulary of other calls including a Whitethroat-like nasal 'churr', a grating *Acrocephalus*-like 'churr' and various jittery rattles (covering BWP 4b, 5b and 5c).

The systematics of the Lesser Whitethroat group are complex and have been reappraised recently. King (1998) reports the research of Martens and Steil recognising 3 groups: the taiga subspecies (*curruca*, *blythi* etc.), the desert subspecies (*minula*, *jaxarctica* and *margelanica*) and the mountain subspecies (*althaea* and *monticola*). Shirihai et al. (2001) treat the group as a superspecies consisting of 4 allospecies, regarding *margelanica* as equally distinct from *minula*. Judging by descriptions in reports (e.g. Birding World 12:7, 13:11, 14:1), suspected eastern birds can be very difficult to identify to race.

Differences in song between allospecies were found to be significant in Martens and Steil's research: *curruca* birds in Germany reacted less to playback of songs of *minula* and *althaea* than to other *curruca*. There was no difference in their response to playback of the songs of local individuals and *curruca* birds from the eastern end of their range.

According to Shirihai et al. the song of *minula* is richer, less stereotyped and possibly homologous to the first part of *curruca* song; song of *althaea* is intermediate between *minula* and *curruca*. The song of *halimodendri* is said to have a repetitive trill like *curruca*. Given that nominate *curruca* birds occasionally sing verses consisting of only the warble or twitter form and that the warble form is dominant in certain sexual contexts, it could be misleading to compare nominate song with limited or isolated observations of eastern birds singing, particularly on passage when subsong may be more usual. A strong familiarity with the songs of the eastern birds would be necessary to use song as a criterion in the identity of eastern birds found beyond their normal range.

Shirihai et al. also report slight differences in the calls of the allospecies: *minula* is thought to have a more grating 'churr' or rattle than *curruca*, whereas *althaea* has a more relaxed, softer rattle. A bird identified as a Desert Lesser Whitethroat on Teesside in 2000 was reported to have distinctive calls: a tit-like *Parus* 'dzjerr dzjerr dzjerr' and a more Wren-like *Troglodytes troglodytes* 'trrr-tic' (Money 2000). A bird in Sweden the same year, showing characteristics of *halimodendri* and *minula* in the hand, was heard to give a similar call, a rapid series of 'che' or 'dze' sounds - 'dze-ze-ze-ze', recalling Blue Tit *P. caeruleus* or Tree Sparrow *Passer montanus* (Pettersen 2001). How these

differ from similar calls of the nominate race in recordings C1 and C2 is not clear: there are few recordings of the eastern allospecies and there's still much to learn about the vocal variation in the group.

Recordings:

3: 49 Song
    1 Northumberland, UK. 23.6.1995 5:00am.
    2 Bialowieza, Poland. 25.5.2002 9:00am.
    3 Northumberland, UK. 15.5.1997 7:00am.

3: 50 Calls
    1 Northumberland, U.K. 5.8.2001 7:30am. Adult probably in vicinity of nest site or fledged young.
    2 Bresse, France. 23.5.1997 6:30am. 3 birds in scrub: probably 2 males and 1 female.

3: 51 ID

COMMON WHITETHROAT
Sylvia communis

STATUS: SUMMER VISITOR TO MUCH OF EUROPE INTO CENTRAL ASIA.
SONG: IN SHORT WARBLED VERSES: SCRATCHY OR CHIRRUPY JANGLE, FAST AND QUITE TUNEFUL.
SONG SEASON: APRIL TO AUGUST (EUROPE).
CALLS: A SHORT NASAL 'CHURR' AND A RISING WHEEZY 'DWEEP'.
CONFUSION SPECIES: OTHER *SYLVIA*, STONECHAT, WHINCHAT.

In terms of the form of their vocalisations and their vocal behaviour, there are similarities between Whitethroats and some of the *Sylvia* warblers of the Mediterranean. Shirihai et al. (2001) treat Common Whitethroat as a separate branch of a common subgeneric grouping with the Mediterranean warblers. All share a preference for rather dry scrub habitats.

Often birds may be encountered in groups after breeding and on migration but they are reported as solitary in winter, when low intensity song is heard. Breeding is territorial and pairs are mainly monogamous, though a small percentage of males are bigamous, both simultaneously with first mate and successively (Cramp et al. 1992).

Males sing from within cover, from low prominent perches, typically the top of a hedge, and sometimes from the crown of a low tree. Every so often they launch into a fluttering song-flight, rising maybe 3–6m before descending to a different song-post; the bird in recording S1 made 1 song-flight every 10–20 verses.

Song from unpaired males can be heard all day long, beginning around dawn and with high output during the morning. Song-flights are reported only to be made once the sun has risen and reach a peak in the late morning (various in Cramp et al.).

Balsby (2000) distinguishes 3 types of song in Whitethroats: the standard form of perched song is a fast warble in fairly brief verses, each opening with a clearer phrase before breaking into a scratchy stuttering. The ending is abrupt. The character on song-flight is rather different, forming a fluid, continuous burst of clear-toned, more melodious phrases (sounding quite like Blackcap). The third type of song the author calls 'diving' song – less obvious and directed at females. I have numerous recordings of birds singing 'excitedly' for quite long periods, usually within cover, in the style of the song-flight, which I take to be Balsby's third type; it may be less obvious than normal song, but the voice is just as loud.

It seems that the output level of perched and flight songs falls when a male gains a mate. Balsby found that in mated males the 'scharp' call (or 'churr' BWP 6c) was the most frequent vocalisation; the author infers a 'silent strategy' from the more discreet vocal behaviour of mated males. Unpaired males typically keep singing until late in the breeding season (Cramp et al.).

Although functionally there may be justification for recognising 3 types of song, from a listener's perspective it's probably more convenient to reduce this to 2, differing in structure: firstly the normal, rather stereotyped verses of perched song and secondly the sweet, varied, Blackcap-like warble of the song-flight and Balsby's 'diving song', which has also been called ecstatic song (e.g. Shirihai et al.). There are elements of mimicry in normal song (often the last syllable), but it is much more frequent in ecstatic song. Although there's variation in the songs I've heard and recorded through Europe, those I've recorded in

Northumberland sound particularly similar to each other, so it may be that local groups of birds share part of their repertoire of motifs or even song-types.

There are 2 commonly heard calls in spring and summer and a variety of less frequently heard ones: the rising, wheezy 'dweep' of recording C2 (BWP 3a, 'wheet' in Cramp et al., 'void' in Balsby) and the short 'churr' in alarm of recording C1 (BWP 6c), similar in tone to Dartford Warbler and variously described in the literature as buzzing or nasal. Calling behaviour is usually skulking, in low to medium height scrub, with just an occasional, brief, stretching look out from an outer twig. More rarely 'tek' calls (BWP 6a, recording C3) and rattles are given in alarm.

Recordings:

3: 52 Song
  1 Bialowieza, Poland. 26.5.2002 7:30am. Edited; with 2 song-flights.
  2 Northumberland, UK. 5.5.2002 6:00am.
  3 Bresse, France. 23.5.1997 5:45am. Mixed style singing; like Blackcap.
  4 Northumberland, UK. 2.5.2002 9:00am. 'Ecstatic' song.

3: 53 Calls
  1 'churr': Cambridge, Oxford & Northumberland, UK. June, July, May.
  2 'dweep': Northumberland, UK. & Bresse, France. May.
  3 Northumberland, UK. 13.7.1997 6:00am. Alarm probably in vicinity of nest or young.

3: 54 ID

GARDEN WARBLER *Sylvia borin*

STATUS: SUMMER VISITOR TO MUCH OF EUROPE.
SONG: A BUBBLING WARBLE, AT A STEADY, FAST PACE; IN VARIABLE LENGTH VERSES WITH SHORT PAUSES.
SONG SEASON: MAINLY APRIL TO JULY.
CALLS: USUALLY IN ALARM A REPEATED, COARSE 'CHEK, CHEK, CHEK...'.
CONFUSION SPECIES: BLACKCAP, WHITETHROAT, BARRED WARBLER.

Garden Warblers are generally skulking birds throughout the year, other than scolding in alarm or males occasionally singing from a prominent perch. Usually solitary in winter and on migration, territorial in the breeding season, pairs are mainly monogamous, though Cramp et al. (1992) report occasional successive polygyny.

Males sometimes sing from a single perch for fairly long periods, particularly at dawn, but more often they deliver one or a few verses on a pause before continuing foraging through shrubbery. For a static bout of song they may find a prominent perch at the top of a small tree or bush, but for much of the time they are a voice without a body, emanating from within the foliage of bushes and shrubs. Birds have been observed singing in flight, usually associated with the proximity of a female or another male, but no true song-flight has been noted (Cramp et al.).

Song output is high in the early morning, during pair-formation and nest-site selection, but can be heard at any time of day throughout the breeding season. Some low intensity song is heard occasionally in late summer to autumn, more regularly in winter quarters, increasing in output and intensity from spring passage.

Full song is usually given in short verses of 3–5 seconds length. Occasionally verses are extended into a more continuous warble; I have a verse of over 30 seconds recorded. The 25 minutes of continuous song reported in Simms (1985) and quoted in Cramp et al. seems to refer to verses separated by very short pauses. In the passages of continuous warbling that I've heard of over about 30 seconds the character of the song changes to a kind of subsong, but loud, and rather different in character from the subsong described in Cramp et al.

This other style of song includes an excited more lightweight warble in territorial and sexual encounters, as in recording S4 with a very Blackcap quality, and passages of a kind of falsetto wheezing, as in recording S5. I've come across a bird newly arrived on breeding grounds singing in a kind of transitional way between subsong and song, but this was in verses, some of which were very Blackcap-like in character. Cramp et al. report a soft courtship song given by both male and female, described as 'chirpy and discontinuous'. An aberrant song said to occur widely in Europe has a rolling, trilling sound, like Alpine Swift *Apus melba*.

The tempo of the phrasing is usually steady and fast, almost doubling up the beat on Barred Warbler, and compared to Blackcap all the syllables, or individual notes, are short. The rhythm of the phrasing in Blackcap song is more varied and broken, with slight pauses used where Garden Warbler seems to flow uninterrupted.

The timbre of the voice varies in song from slightly grating or buzzy 'churr's, through full lower-pitched, slightly trilled whistles (like Mistle Thrush *Turdus viscivorus*) to clearer-toned, high slurred whistles. These latter are very similar to Blackcap song, though the clear-toned whistles are a more dominant component in Blackcap, particularly in the later part of a verse. Garden Warbler is often described as mellow (Cramp et al.), where I find Blackcap full song rather strident and higher-pitched.

There's some evidence of interspecific territorial competition with Barred Warbler, Whitethroat and Blackcap, though Blackcaps are more responsive to playback of Garden Warbler song (Cramp et al.).

Garden Warbler song is often riddled with mimicry, particularly Blackbird *Turdus merula*, Chaffinch *Fringilla coelebs* and, in Britain at least, Dunnock *Prunella modularis*, but it often passes unnoticed, because of the pace of the delivery and the short snatches of the imitations.

The most regularly heard call, though not frequent, is a coarse 'chek', lower in pitch and given singly in contact, rising in pitch and intensity when alarmed, and repeated in series. It's a slightly longer note than the tongue-clicking call of many of its congeners; the length, coarse timbre and rapid, regular repetition are fairly diagnostic. Cramp et al. also describe various rasping, churring and rattling calls reported for situations of dispute and sexual excitement. The strange bubbling churr, just audible in recording C3, may fall into this category or may be another alarm call.

Recordings:
3: 55 Song
    1 Northumberland, UK. 10.7.1999 8:00am. Blackcap in background.
    2 Bresse, France. 22.5.1997 6:45am.
    3 Biebrza, Poland. 20.5.2002 3:30pm. Two males singing close.
    4 Inverness-shire, UK. 12.6.1992

6:30am.

3: 56   Calls

1   Northumberland, UK. 15.6.2000
    1:30pm.

2   Northumberland, UK. 15.6.2000
    3:00pm. Different bird from previous.

3   Northumberland, UK. 4.7.1999
    9:30am.

3: 57   ID

BLACKCAP *Sylvia atricapilla*

STATUS: SUMMER VISITOR TO NORTH AND EAST
EUROPE, PARTIAL MIGRANT IN SOUTH AND WEST.
SONG: IN VERSES THAT BUILD FROM A HESITANT
OPENING TO RICH FLUTEY PHRASINGS, OFTEN
PROLONGED.
SONG SEASON: MAINLY APRIL TO JULY.
CALLS: A CLASSIC TONGUE-CLICKING 'TEK' OR
'TCHK'.
CONFUSION SPECIES: GARDEN WARBLER,
WHITETHROAT.

Blackcap is a popular singer among British birders
and a favourite for many. With a varied and musical
song it provides a welcome front-line melody to many
a woodland and scrubland chorus. I find Blackcap's
voice a little strident sometimes and generally prefer
the more mellow sound of Garden Warbler. But I've
just listened through my Blackcap song recordings and
really I'd forgotten just how good a singer Blackcap
can be; but not all the time: there are long passages of
birds singing rather tightly-structured verses with no
real sparkle in the phrasing (to my ears!). So bear in
mind that the recordings I've used tend to be the more
exciting singers.

Breeding is almost always monogamous and males
usually stay till the young are independent (Cramp et
al. 1992). On arrival in breeding area, males may be
silent at first; they may wander an area widely without
defending it (possibly 1-year-olds), defend a larger
pre-territory or sometimes occupy the fixed breeding
territory (maybe older birds).

Typically they have favourite song-posts, prominent
if not conspicuous, often at mid-height, probably
rather higher on average than Garden Warbler, as
might be expected of the more arboreal species. But

birds will also sing low down from within cover,
usually a less structured, more continuous song,
especially early in the breeding season, possibly when
a female is about – i.e. courtship song (recording S3).
Song in flight is rare other than approaching an
intruder on territory (Garcia in Cramp et al.); song
duels frequently occur in territorial disputes.

Peak song output is early in the breeding season
during territory establishment and pair formation,
particularly in the early morning and to a lesser extent
at dusk, though birds can be heard throughout the day.
There's a resurgence of song before a second brood,
otherwise late singers are thought to be unpaired birds
(Simms 1985). Subsong is sometimes heard in the
autumn, increasing to a fuller song from wintering
birds in the south of the range towards spring. Song
has occasionally been heard from apparent females,
usually sounding like male subsong (Cramp et al.); an
apparent female recorded by David Lumsdaine
(personal communication) sang in the same style as a
more rambling male song.

Full song typically is in verses with short intervals,
that build from a hesitant jumble of thin and scratchy
notes into more fluent phrasing in a clear fluting
whistle, ending with a distinct motif. The fluted
phrases towards the end reach full volume and tend to
be more stereotyped than the first part; individuals
have a few favourite endings which they use regularly.
Shirihai et al. (2001) quote Svensson that birds of an
area share the same endings which thus form
recognisable local dialects.

Males may sing in this form for long periods,
sometimes moving a short way between verses, then
moving on to a new song-post. Birds singing the
continuous, rambling style (courtship and excitement
songs (1b) in Cramp et al.) tend to remain perched in
cover; this is still in more or less full voice, fluent and
with well-enunciated phrases, so strictly speaking not
what is usually understood by subsong. Softer subsong
is also given all year round, but is more noticeable
outside the main breeding season.

Compared with Garden Warbler, Blackcap song has
more articulated and varied phrasing, with variations
in pace and rhythm. Verses end in a flourish, usually a
recognisable motif. In the syllables of Blackcap song
purer tones predominate in comparison to Garden
Warbler's bubbling 'burr'. The purer tones and higher

song-posts mean that Blackcap song generally carries a little further than that of Garden Warbler.

Continuous song and the introductory part of full song frequently include mimicry of other species; the imitations are often phrases of song from other species rather than just calls, which tend to predominate in *Acrocephalus* songs. Quite a wide range of species is imitated (see Simms), with thrush *Turdus* rather frequent; I've come across several birds in Northumberland that seemed to be particularly influenced by neighbouring Song Thrushes *T. philomelos* (recording S4, with the Song Thrush model itself in the background).

It has been suggested that song is deeper in the south of its range (Chappuis in Cramp et al.) and other consistently distinct geographical variants have been proposed, such as a particular modified ending in central Europe (Sauer in Simms). The song in recording S5, with a very distinctive 2-note phrase, may be the 'Leiern-variant' discussed fully in Shirihai et al. They also regard the apparent mimicry of Lesser Spotted Woodpecker *Dendrocopos minor* (Curber 1969) and Wryneck *Jynx torquilla* calls (Paull 1977) as songs of this variant type.

The main contact and alarm call is a classic *Sylvia* tongue-clicking 'tak', 'teck' (Mullarney et al. 1999) or 'tacc' (Shirihai et al.), rapidly repeated in alarm or excitement (BWP 4a). Note how the adult's alarm silences the young in recording C5. Another common alarm call is a variable, rasping or squeaky 'zeur' ('dzaaak', Shirihai et al.; 'sweer', Witherby in Cramp et al., BWP 4b) as in recording C3, probably because of Magpie *Pica pica* nearby. Other calls heard occasionally include wheezy whistles (which may be variants of previous), mewing and churring sounds (Cramp et al.). Simms also reports low gurgles amongst mated pairs, croaking calls from aggressive males and strident yells at ground predators.

Lesser Whitethroat's main call is very similar to that of Blackcap, but slightly lower-pitched and with a more lip-smacking or sucking timbre, but note the fledgling calls in recording C4 also have something of this quality. This recording also suggests that the fledgling

call, 'sieb' ending in a loose 'chak' ('idat', Bergmann in Cramp et al.), may become the mewing call described for adults. The suggestion that the 'dat' ending later develops into the adult call appears to be at odds with this juvenile also giving a version of the adult call.

Recordings:
3: 58 Song
1   Sussex, UK. 1.5.1993 6:30am.
2   Provence, France. 1.6.1997 7:00am. Singer conspicuous at 2m height.
3   Northumberland, UK. 26.4.1998 2:30pm. Singer in low scrub; female nearby.
4   Northumberland, UK. 4.7.1999 9:00am. Singing and moving; Song Thrush mimicry.
5   Northumberland, UK. 25.5.1995 7:00pm. Leiern variant.
3: 59 Calls
1   Northumberland, UK. 25.9.2000 4:00pm.
2   Northumberland, UK. 4.7.1999 10:00am. Female.
3   Sussex, UK. 1.5.1993 6:30am.
4   Northumberland, UK. 5.6.1998 3:30pm. Newly-fledged young on ground.
5   Provence, France. 30.5.1997 9:00pm. Suspected family party.
3: 60 ID

PHYLLOSCOPUS

GREEN WARBLER
Phylloscopus trochiloides nitidus

STATUS: SUMMER VISITOR TO CAUCASUS REGION AND NEARBY.
SONG: IN SHORT VERSES OF TWITTERING PHRASES; REPETITIVE AND EVEN PACED.
SONG SEASON: MAY TO JULY.
CALLS: VERY LIKE GREENISH: A SIBILANT, DISYLLABIC 'CHE-WE'.
CONFUSION SPECIES: GREENISH WARBLER, TWO-BARRED GREENISH WARBLER.

Considered by Cramp et al. (1992) as a separate species close in form and behaviour to Greenish Warbler, Mullarney et al. (1999) treat this species as a 'rather well-marked race of Greenish Warbler, close to being a full species'. Often encountered in loose flocks after breeding and on autumn passage, Green Warbler has been reported as solitary in winter and a territorial breeder, though there's no information on pairing system (Cramp et al.).

Males sing from a perch, high in available trees or bushes, sometimes for long periods (10–15 minutes) and also moving between verses; song has not been noted in flight and Green Warbler is reported as not quite so restless as Greenish (P.S.Hansen in Cramp et al.). Singing is said to be intensive as soon as birds arrive on breeding grounds from late April.

The species or race is very similar vocally to Greenish Warbler. Song is in rather short verses composed of a repetitive series of high-pitched phrases (pitch as Greenish) in a sweet sibilant voice. The songs on recordings I've heard have been at a slightly slower tempo, without the accelerations of Greenish song, and possibly fuller voiced or in more articulated phrases. There's also a tendency to alternate high and low notes. The staccato rhythms, repetitive phrasing and overall tone are quite reminiscent of Cetti's Warbler song.

The main contact and alarm call is a brief but markedly disyllabic 'chi-wee', varying in voicing and barely distinguishable from the calls of Greenish.

Recordings:
1: 28 Song
K.Mild. North-east Turkey. May 1991.
1: 29 Calls
P.Holt/NSA. Kerala, India. 5.1.1995 noon.
1: 30 ID

GREENISH WARBLER
Phylloscopus trochiloides viridanus

STATUS: SUMMER VISITOR TO NORTH-EAST EUROPE AND INTO ASIA.
SONG: A BRISK SERIES OF SING-SONG PHRASES, IN A CHIFFCHAFF-LIKE VOICE, ENDING IN A TWITTER.
SONG SEASON: MAINLY MAY TO JULY.
CALLS: A RATHER SIBILANT, DISYLLABIC 'CHI-WEE'.
CONFUSION SPECIES: COAL TIT (SONG); PIED/WHITE WAGTAIL (CALLS).

Overall from descriptions and recordings listened to, it appears there's quite extensive variation in both the structure and voicing of the song and calls, which makes it difficult to identify diagnostic characteristics in Green, Greenish and Two-barred Greenish Warbler vocalisation. Though the song is described as variable (across random individuals and instances), it appears that groups of males in any area use a limited repertoire of rather stereotyped songs (Cramp et al. 1992) and it may be that familiarity with song-types is necessary to attempt vocal subspecific identification.

The voice in all 3 races or species has regularly been compared with wagtails *Motacilla*, flycatchers *Ficedula* and Coal Tit *Parus ater*, particularly White or Pied Wagtail *M. alba*, This holds true for the timbre and twittering character of the song, but more so for the calls, very similar in form to this wagtail species' calls.

Though encountered in small parties on passage, territorial defence and song is noted from birds of both sexes in their wintering areas. The breeding system appears to be monogamous. Birds are reported to be typically restless in their movements, but not particularly shy of humans (Cramp et al.).

Song is usually delivered while a bird pauses during foraging high up in tree foliage, sometimes lower down and sometimes remaining in one spot for a series of verses (up to 5 minutes: Schüz in Cramp et al.). Birds may sing in flight, but there appears to be no ritualised song-flight. Song output peaks at the start of the breeding season and declines during nesting with a resumption on fledging of the young. Males can be heard singing throughout the day from soon after sunrise, but the song-rate generally appears to be higher in the morning than the afternoon (max. c.10 songs per minute).

Song is in verses of a vigorous, high-pitched series of rhythmic phrases; delivery is at a brisk pace, with the syllables reminiscent of Chiffchaff in timbre and form. Cramp et al. emphasise a final trilled phrase recalling Wren *Troglodytes troglodytes* or Wood Warbler; the bird in recording S1 seems to lack this or have a rather rudimentary version, as do other recordings of *viridanus*, the western race, I've listened to, whereas there's a trill ending to some of the songs in Green Warbler recording S1.

The Greenish songs heard on several recordings begin with roughly the same phrasing '(ti-)ti-chow-chow-ti-chow...' leading into faster twittered phrasing; the introductory syllables sound very similar to the usual call. The accelerating phrases give a structure like Chaffinch *Fringilla coelebs* song. The hint of sibilance in the timbre and the lively rhythm of the phrasing generate the similarity to Coal Tit, though verse structure differs.

The usual call, heard all year round, is a very Pied Wagtail-like 'chi-wee'; the alternative rendering 'tiss-yip' suggests its sibilant timbre. Normally disyllabic, 'jaded' variations may lose much of the second syllable and other voicings suggest a more complex structure, evident on analysis. Recording C1 includes variations and a distinctly monosyllabic 'tsee'. Other occasional or context-specific calls include a low 'trrr' given as warning.

In the recording of Greenish song on Roché (1993), the bird gives a terse 'chit' call before each delivery, which may be part of the verse or may be a very basic interstrophic call, though other reports note a quiet, high-pitched 'si' as occasionally given between verses (Schüz, Schubert in Cramp et al.)

Autumn vagrants in western Europe have been heard to call, mostly in the early morning (G.Sangster in Cramp et al.) and sing occasionally.

Recordings:

1: 31　Song
　　　　V.Runnel. Southern Estonia. 2.6.2001.
1: 32　Calls
　　　　P.Holt/NSA. Eastern Nepal. 16.1.1997
　　　　11:30am
1: 33　ID

TWO-BARRED GREENISH WARBLER
Phylloscopus trochiloides plumbeitarsus

The song of this eastern race of Greenish Warbler in recording S1 differs from that of *viridanus* in eastern Europe in being more hurried, less clearly articulated and lacking the twittered ending. It's also at an appreciably more hurried pace than the songs of Green Warbler. The call is still disyllabic and Pied Wagtail-like, but possibly fuller-voiced and less sibilant or 'frothy'.

How consistent these differences are for other Two-barred *plumbeitarsus* individuals and other groups of *trochiloides*, I can't say.

Recordings:

1: 34　Song
　　　　P.Holt/NSA. Hebei, China. 23.5.1996
　　　　5:30am.
1: 35　Calls
　　　　As for song.
1: 36　ID

ARCTIC WARBLER *Phylloscopus borealis*

STATUS: SUMMER VISITOR TO NORTHERN EUROPE AND ASIA.
SONG: VERSES OF A TRILL, SIMILAR TO BONELLI'S WARBLERS, BUT LONGER.
SONG SEASON: JUNE TO JULY (SCANDINAVIA).
CALLS: AN ABRUPT 'DZIK', WITH A METALLIC BUZZ LIKE DIPPER.
CONFUSION SPECIES: BUNTINGS? (CALL).

Wintering in south-east Asia, Scandinavian birds have a long journey and are late in arriving on the breeding grounds, normally from the second half of

June. Arctic Warblers are often encountered in groups of family parties after breeding and with mixed flocks on autumn passage, otherwise in winter mostly solitary or in pairs. Breeding is thought to be mainly monogamous, though some bigamy has been recorded (Cramp et al. 1992).

Males sing from a high perch, typically a tree top, and sometimes from within foliage, for periods up to 1 hour from the same perch (Blair in Cramp et al.). They have a wing-flapping display, performed perched, and sometimes give an unusual wing-rattling sound in flight between song-posts. Studies in various areas report different diurnal patterns for singing and, as well as morning, it seems many birds sing in the evening and some at night. Song output is thought to be highest when they first arrive on the breeding grounds and song is sometimes heard from migrants.

Song is in verses of a loud trill (2–4 seconds long), each sounding of more or less the same syllable, though drifting a little in pitch. The timbre is similar to Bonelli's Warblers, but the longer verse makes it reminiscent of Cirl Bunting *Emberiza cirlus*, though not quite so dry. The opening builds in volume and the syllables, or units, of the trill prove to be quite complex on analysis, revealing greater variation within an individual's song-type repertoire than is easily perceived with our hearing. Often birds repeat the main call, though a little quieter, between verses – the *Phylloscopus* interstrophic call.

The usual contact and alarm call is a sharp 'dzik' or disyllabic 'zirik', varying between individuals and usually given several times in succession. An autumn vagrant in Britain gave this distinctive call occasionally and also gave an aggressive buzz or rattle at another species that came too close (recording C3). The bird in recording C1 gives another call or more probably a variant, 'zwik'; Cramp et al. report variations in other races. Occasional calls include abrupt 'pit's in excitement, low 'churr's or rattles and whirring sounds during copulation.

Recordings:

1: 37 Song
    1   I.Hills/NSA. Norway. 4.7.1977.
    2   P.S.Hansen/NSA. Finland. 5.7.1991.
1: 38 Calls
    1   As S1 above.

    2   As S2 above.
    3   Northumberland, UK. 15.9.2002 6:30pm.
1: 39 ID

PALLAS'S WARBLER
Phylloscopus proregulus

STATUS: VAGRANT (MAINLY AUTUMN) TO EUROPE.
SONG: IN VARIABLE LENGTH BURSTS OF A RICH, SWEET WARBLE AT A BRISK PACE.
SONG SEASON: OCCASIONAL ON PASSAGE AND IN WINTER.
CALLS: A SWEET 'CHUEE', SECOND SYLLABLE RISING ABRUPTLY; OR JUST 'CHEW'.
CONFUSION SPECIES: YELLOW-BROWED WARBLER, HUME'S LEAF WARBLER, GREENISH WARBLER.

Cramp et al. (1992) report Pallas's as generally less vocal than Yellow-browed, though song is heard on migration and in winter and both song and calls have been heard from vagrants in Europe. The song is said to be loud, rich and varied, with something of the character of Willow Warbler though faster and with Wren-like *Troglodytes troglodytes* trilling.

Calls may be rather varied (cf recordings) but tend to be short rather delicately articulated monosyllabic and disyllabic notes in a voice reminiscent of Chiffchaff. Most frequent are various rather sweet 'chew' or 'chewee' notes, but they also include a high 'tee' or 'swee' and a more explosive 'tchi'. When the 'chewee' note is voiced thinly, the sound approaches that of Hume's or Yellow-browed.

This Northumberland bird called regularly in coastal scrub with small trees and delivered snatches of song, probably more rambling than full song, late on a sunny morning. Pallas's Warbler is a regular autumn vagrant to the east coast of Britain. The first spring record for Northumberland involved a singing male at a coastal site on 11th May 2000.

Recordings:

1: 40 Subsong & calls
    Northumberland, UK. 22.10.1999 11:30am.
ID   see 1: 43

YELLOW-BROWED WARBLER
Phylloscopus inornatus

STATUS: REGULAR, THOUGH RARE, AUTUMN VAGRANT TO EUROPE.
SONG: SHORT VERSE LIKE A SERIES OF CALLS.
SONG SEASON: HAS BEEN NOTED FROM AUTUMN VAGRANTS.
CALLS: A THIN, HIGH-PITCHED, DRAWN-OUT 'TSOO-EEST'.
CONFUSION SPECIES: HUME'S LEAF WARBLER, PALLAS'S WARBLER, COAL TIT.

Yellow-browed Warblers are generally considered to be vocal birds, even as autumn vagrants (e.g. Cramp et al., Mullarney et al. 1999), but the few I've watched in Britain haven't called often – e.g. 3 series of c.6 calls in 3 hours. None of them have been as vocal as the 2 Hume's I've watched and recorded, so there is individual variation in their vocal behaviour.

The usual call is distinctive: a thin, though rather explosive 'sweest' (Mullarney et al.), with a slurred, but steep, rise in pitch towards the end; with variations in voicing, sometimes it can sound more disyllabic. Much more sibilant than either Hume's or Pallas's, it's often likened to one of the calls of Coal Tit *Parus ater*.

Song sounds rather rudimentary and little more than a series of simple elaborations on the call.

Recordings:
1: 41 Calls
      1   P.Holt/NSA. Hebei, China.
          10.5.1996 8:00am.
ID   see 1: 43

HUME'S LEAF WARBLER
Phylloscopus humei

STATUS: RARE VAGRANT TO EUROPE.
SONG: A LOOSE MIX OF CALL-NOTES AND A BUZZING WHEEZE.
SONG SEASON: NOT YET NOTED FROM VAGRANTS APPARENTLY.
CALLS: A TERSE 'TSLIEP' OR DISYLLABIC 'TUSS-LIEP'.
CONFUSION SPECIES: YELLOW-BROWED, PALLAS'S WARBLERS.

Hume's Leaf Warbler has only recently been recognised as a full species separate from Yellow-browed Warbler; differences in vocalisation were important criteria in the split and Millington & Mullarney (2000) consider 'calls are the absolute clincher' for identification in the field.

The 2 birds I watched and recorded on the Northumberland coast in the winter of 2001/2002 were both vocal, the long-staying Lynemouth bird very much so. The calls I recorded from the two sound rather different to our ears. Spectrographic analysis suggests that the call in recording C1 is the same as recording C2, but with an added percussive element at the start. This opening element has some higher frequencies that suggest the timbre of Yellow-browed's 'soeest', though clearly different in a side-to-side comparison. This is presumably also the Chiffchaff-like 'weeischb' of Millington & Mullarney.

The calls in the second recording are presumably the diagnostic sparrow-like *Passer* 'dswielp' of Millington & Mullarney and sound clearly different from Yellow-browed's usual call, with a sudden dip in pitch at the end where Yellow-browed's rises. Were these two different birds or two different calls from the same bird? They were about 5 miles and 3 months apart.

Song is said to be a loose arrangement of call-like notes and a buzzing wheeze, something like the 'seeip' call of Redwing *Turdus iliacus* (Svensson in Cramp et al. 1992).

Recordings:
1: 42 Calls
      1   Northumberland, UK. 20.10.2001
          & 23.10.2001. 2 sequences.
      2   Northumberland, UK. 24.1.2002
          & 6.2.2002. 2 sequences.
1: 43 ID Pallas's, Yellow-browed, and Hume's Leaf Warblers.

RADDE'S WARBLER
Phylloscopus schwarzi

STATUS: RARE VAGRANT TO EUROPE.
SONG: IN VERSES OF A LIVELY FLUID TRILL, LIKE BONELLI'S WARBLERS.
CALLS: A LOW 'CHEK' AND A SOFT 'PWIT'.
CONFUSION SPECIES: DUSKY WARBLER.

Calls are described in Madge (1990) as a low, quiet, often irregularly repeated 'chep' and 'chek-chek'. Cramp et al. (1992) also distinguish a soft 'pwit', with a Quail-like *Coturnix coturnix* quality and report this as the most common call of wintering birds. Judging by the recording, where essentially the same call has variations in voicing covering both these descriptions, they may be referring to a single type of call.

The Quail-like timbre is apparent on some of this bird's renditions, but was very marked in the call of a singing bird on another recording in the NSA; the same slightly whiplash quality is also in some *Locustella* calls (e.g. River and Savi's Warblers). In comparison the calls of Dusky Warbler are much closer to Lesser Whitethroat 'tsuk's.

Song is in verses of a rather clear-toned, liquid trill introduced by a couple of call-like notes, the syllables of the trill varying between verses as in Bonelli's Warblers.

Recordings:

1: 44   Calls
P.Holt/NSA. Hebei, China. 10.5.1996
5:30am.
1:46   ID

DUSKY WARBLER *Phylloscopus fuscatus*

STATUS: RARE VAGRANT TO EUROPE.
SONG: IN LOUD, BRIEF VERSES OF REPEATING WHISTLED PHRASES.
CALLS: A SYLVIA-LIKE, LIP-SMACKING 'TSUK'.
CONFUSION SPECIES: *SYLVIA* WARBLERS, WREN, RADDE'S WARBLER.

Rather similar to a Chiffchaff visually, the usual calls are closer to a *Sylvia* tongue-clicking 'tak' than any other *Phylloscopus*. Fortunately autumn vagrants are often quite vocal, giving this call freely. Both birds I've seen were vocal; on the other hand no calls were heard from a bird on the Northumberland coast in November 2000.

The usual and diagnostic call in recording C1 seems most similar to Lesser Whitethroat, but with an even more lip-smacking sound. Song is said to be monotonous in composition, but with clear whistles and chirruping tones (Cramp et al. 1992).

Recordings:

1: 45   Calls
Northumberland, UK. 23.10.2002
11:00am.
1: 46   ID   Radde's and Dusky Warblers.

WESTERN & EASTERN BONELLI'S WARBLERS *Phylloscopus bonelli & Phylloscopus orientalis*

STATUS: SUMMER VISITOR TO SOUTH AND WEST EUROPE.
SONG: A SHORT, MORE OR LESS SIBILANT, LIQUID OR WOODEN TRILL.
SONG SEASON: APRIL TO JUNE OR JULY.
CALLS: AN EMPHATICALLY SLURRED 'CLOY' OR 'CLOY-EU' (*BONELLI*); AN ABRUPT 'CHIP' (*ORIENTALIS*).
CONFUSION SPECIES: WOOD WARBLER, CIRL BUNTING, WILLOW WARBLER.

Bonelli's Warblers are close relatives of Wood Warbler, which they roughly replace to the south; what were regarded as separate races have recently been recognised as distinct species on genetic and vocal differences. Much of the literature previous to this provides a single description for both species and it's not clear how similar they are in behaviour; the Eastern species is not as well known as the Western and my field experience with the Eastern is limited to hearing one bird several hundred metres away up a hillside in Greece.

Birds are reported as solitary and territorial in winter, though often found in loose parties on migration (Cramp et al. 1992). Song can be heard throughout the day at the start of the the breeding season with peaks in the morning and evening. Output is reduced once males are paired and nesting begins, with a resumption once young are fledged, though other studies suggest there may be regional variation in singing patterns. Some song is heard on migration and is reported as frequent in winter. Cramp et al. also suggest song is rare compared with calls in *orientalis* and verses are said to be shorter and less vigorous.

The Bonelli's I recorded in Spain were a pleasure to work with. They came very close on their song circuit through the foliage of short oaks on the steep hillsides, leaving an impression of very active, sleek birds. All the birds I observed and recorded sang while foraging, pausing to deliver usually 1 verse, occasionally a short series of verses; Cramp et al. note singing from a high perch, in a tree crown, as more usual.

The song of *bonelli* is in verses of a brief trill, usually less than a second in length, each a regular repetition (7–13 times) of a single element. Elements vary between verses. Its less sibilant, lower-pitched and much shorter than Wood Warbler and sounds rather closer to Cirl Bunting *Emberiza cirlus*, the trill part of Lesser Whitethroat song and Arctic Warbler. Verses are delivered at a rate of about 7 per minute early in the breeding season. The bird singing in France in June (recording S3) left intervals of 10–15 seconds between verses.

The trills of the birds in Spain (recordings S1 and S2) varied from thin and sibilant, rather Wood Warbler-like elements, to fuller more Cirl Bunting-like. The songs of the bird in France (recording S3) are very similar but with a tendency for the last few elements of the trill to fade, and even fall in pitch.

In the recording of *orientalis* song the verses are of a similar form but the elements are drier and more percussive; one of the song-types is hardly more than a repeated, emphatic call-note and unlike any of the songs I've heard from *bonelli*. Svensson (2002) suggests that *orientalis* is prone to use its call in place of song, unlike *bonelli*.

The main contact and alarm call of *bonelli* is a variable, drawn-out 'cloy-eu', with the second syllable accentuated and pitch falling at the end, or simply just 'cleuy' without the final pitch drop. The rich, slightly flutey tone, though rather nasal, is comparable to Wood Warbler's call, rather than the thinner call of Willow Warbler and even thinner Chiffchaff. Calls may be harsher and more metallic from disturbed birds in the autumn (Cramp et al.); they report various other calls heard occasionally in antagonistic, courtship and breeding contexts, ranging from sharp monosyllables to ticking and other repetitions.

The diagnostic call for *orientalis* and the real clincher is a short chirp or 'chip', quite distinct from *bonelli*, and usually compared with sparrow *Passer* or Crossbill *Loxia curvirostra* (e.g. Cramp et al., page 1999). Svensson notes a subdued 'isst', related to the 'chip' call, from migrant *orientalis* birds, where migrant *bonelli* are usually silent.

There was some confusion about the calls of the first *orientalis* bird for Britain. The observers assumed that a strident disyllabic 'hooeet' call they heard was from the same bird which had been observed giving the distinctive 'chip'. Since this call has never otherwise been heard from *orientalis*, it's now thought that the 'hooect' must have been from a different bird (Wilson & Fentiman 1999). If *orientalis* should have a 'hooeet' call, it would make it very difficult to separate these species in the field.

Recordings:
Western Bonelli's Warbler *P. bonelli*
1: 47 Song
    1   Valencia, Spain. 15.4.2001 11:30am.
    2   Valencia, Spain. 21.4.2001 9:00am.
    3   Languedoc, France. 6.6.1997 9:15pm.
1: 48 Calls
    1   Valencia, Spain. 15.4.2001 noon.
    2   Valencia, Spain. 24.4.2001 12:30pm.
1: 49 ID

Eastern Bonelli's Warbler *P. orientalis*
1: 50 Song
    C.J.Hazevoet/NSA. Noord-Hollannd,
    Netherlands. 15.5.1983 7:30pm.
1: 51 Calls
    As S1.
1: 52 ID

WOOD WARBLER *Phylloscopus sibilatrix*

STATUS: SUMMER VISITOR TO MUCH OF EUROPE, ONLY ON PASSAGE IN THE IBERIAN PENINSULA.
SONG: IN VERSES OF A PROTRACTED, RATHER SIBILANT, ECSTATIC TRILL, INTERSPERSED WITH OCCASIONAL SERIES OF 'DÜÜ' NOTES.
SONG SEASON: MAY TO JUNE.
CALLS: A RICH, PLAINTIVE 'DÜÜ', SIMILAR TO THE ALTERNATIVE SONG.
CONFUSION SPECIES: BONELLI'S WARBLERS?

Birds are reported as solitary or in small groups in winter and on migration; song is heard occasionally, particularly on spring migration, but no territorial behaviour has been noted (Cramp et al. 1992).

Although pairs are generally monogamous, most males attempt to attract a second female, with 50% of males polygynous in an exceptional year in Sweden (Temrin 1986). Temrin found that male song output declined on acquiring a mate and birds sang short songs; after a few days they began singing long songs in a far part of their territory or in a secondary territory to try to attract a second female.

Males arrive before females and begin to sing in a favourite display and singing area within their territories. Birds sing from medium to high perches, usually well beneath tree canopy, often moving between verses; song is also given in horizontal, slow-motion flight between perches with vibrating wings. Temrin found that whenever a female entered a male's display area, song virtually ceased. The main song period is through May and June, more occasional in July and from early birds arriving in April. Song can be heard throughout the day early in the breeding season.

The song is in verses of a drawn-out sibilant or even metallic trill, usually in 2 parts with slightly different syllables: the first accelerates from a few quiet opening notes, growing in loudness before transforming into a fast, even trill, the whole thing usually lasting 3 to 4 seconds. The song is fairly stereotyped within individuals, though each verse has a range of variation in the syllables, comparable to the variation between verses in Bonelli's Warblers. After pairing, often only an abbreviated trill song is given in the vicinity of the female (May & Manning 1951). There are reports of birds singing aberrant songs including one like Greenish Warbler (Mikkola in Cramp et al.).

The syllables of the song cover a rather wide band of higher frequencies and, when heard in a forest community, Wood Warbler songs fill a large slice of the available frequency spectrum. They can be heard at up to 400m, ringing out in the sub-canopy acoustic. At peak output birds sing about 7 verses per minute.

The alternative song, a series of call-like notes, is mainly given by males in full song (i.e. unpaired birds and birds singing to attract a second female), occasionally interspersed in an interval between trilling songs (1 to every 5–12 trill songs, Nicholson & Koch in Cramp et al.). The voicing is more fluted and piping in these song-notes than those given as calls. Might this alternative song be the relic of an interstrophic call (cf Willow Warbler and Chiffchaff), that over time has become the structural equivalent of a verse?

The main alarm and contact call is similar to the 'düü' or 'pew' notes of the alternative song, with a timbre reminiscent of Bullfinch *Pyrrhula pyrrhula*; often the voicing is slightly thinner, sounding nearer to 'tee' in alarm (cf recording C1). The bird in recording C2 also gives a disyllabic variant; this was probably a female since there was a male singing in the vicinity.

Other calls heard occasionally include a shrill 'see-see-see' from excited males, repeated 'chk' or 'wit' notes around the nest and hissing sounds in various contexts.

Recordings:

1: 53 Song
   1 Bialowieza, Poland. 27.5.2002 6:00am.
   2 Inverness-shire, UK. 8.6.1992 6:00am.
   3 Bialowieza, Poland. 25.5.2002 10:00am.
   Songs with long intros.

1: 54 Calls
   1 Inverness-shire, UK. 16.6.1992 12:30pm.
   2 Biebrza, Poland. 20.5.2002 8:00am. Probably female.

1: 55 ID

CHIFFCHAFF *Phylloscopus collybita*

STATUS: SUMMER VISITOR AND PARTIAL MIGRANT IN EUROPE.
SONG: AN EVEN-PACED SERIES OF 'CHIFF' NOTES, VARIED BUT AT A FAIRLY CONSTANT PITCH.
SONG SEASON: MAINLY MARCH TO JULY, BUT CAN BE HEARD IN ANY MONTH.
CALLS: USUALLY A RISING 'TWEEP', RATHER SQUEAKY.
CONFUSION SPECIES: WILLOW WARBLER (CALLS).

Although its common name is undoubtedly onomatopoeic, it shouldn't be read too strictly: out of all my recordings of song from 9 different birds, different areas, different years, not one sings with a regular two-note lilt. All sing a very even-tempoed series of 'chiff'-like syllables, but with slight variations.

There's great interest in Chiffchaff vocalisation, since without hearing their voice, they are not easy birds to identify. Song is easy to recognise since, at least for the nominate race, there is no other species song like it; calls are a little more difficult, but generally unmistakable for a good ear with a bit of practice.

The species complex has a wide range, stretching from the Iberian peninsula through to eastern Siberia. Birders have long recognised slight visual differences and greater vocal differences between groups – particularly the Iberian form (*brehmii*), the Mountain or Caucasian Chiffchaff (*sindianus*), the Siberian form (*tristis*) and the isolated Canary Islands Chiffchaff (*canariensis*). Recent research using DNA analysis and voice comparisons has prompted the British Ornithologists' Union to accept all these forms as different species except the Siberian, whose taxonomic status proved difficult. The Scandinavian form (*abietinus*), along with Siberian, has been retained within the nominate taxon and seems to present a clinal variation from birds similar to the nominate in the west to paler and greyer birds, similar to Siberian, in the east. Vinicombe (2000) discusses the relationship and identification of the 3 northern forms.

For us in the UK Chiffchaffs are the first migrant warbler to return and sing; usually the first song is heard in March even in northern England. A few, possibly unmated birds, continue singing into July, then there is a slight resurgence of song in the late summer and autumn, especially on sunny mornings. Song is heard occasionally during the winter months in southern England (Beckerlegge 1951).

Song is usually given from within the canopy of trees or scrub, occasionally from a more exposed perch in the outer foliage; birds tend to sing a verse, move on foraging, then stop to sing the next verse. Cramp et al. (1992) also report occasional snatches of song from females, regularly by one bird on approach to nest, and subsong. Breeding is mainly monogamous, with some polygyny in dense populations.

The song of the nominate *collybita* form is in verses of a slow and steady series of 'chiff'-like syllables, each usually varying slightly. Verses are normally between 2–5 seconds long, sometimes up to 15 seconds, once 48 seconds (Brown et al. 1950 in Cramp et al.), with the intervals between verses usually 4–10 seconds.

Males may repeat a short, dry 'tret' call between song verses (interstrophic), made up of 2 or 3 elements (BWP 5a). This is heard more often early in the breeding season, though sometimes through to July.

In a study using playback, McGregor (1988) found that difference in song length between males was significant and might be a sign of male 'quality'. Playback tended to elicit shorter songs in response (as with Willow Warbler and Great Reed Warbler), suggesting shorter songs sufficed for male to male territorial signalling.

A few authors continue to describe the main contact and alarm call of Chiffchaff as a disyllabic 'hoo-eet', which I think is misleading. The main risk of confusion is with the equivalent call of Willow Warbler and to some extent the 'rain call' of Chaffinch *Fringilla coelebs* ('weet'); but Willow Warbler's call is emphatically inflected, where that of Chiffchaff is a continuously rising note, hence I feel it's more accurate to describe the Willow call as disyllabic. Occasionally you come across a Chiffchaff with a slightly more prolonged call, approaching the form of the Willow, then the other characteristic becomes important: Chiffchaff calls have something of the timbre of a squeaky toy, with sometimes a hint of sibilant wheeziness. Willow Warbler calls in a more rounded whistle.

In late summer and autumn, at least here on the north-east coast of Britain, variations on this main call are heard, often an inflected 'sweeoo' or just plain 'swee' (recordings C3 and C4). These appear to be from birds drifting south, maybe juveniles, though described in Cramp et al. as 'apparently mainly a long-retained juvenile call, but also given by adults'. I've heard birds uttering the normal call switch to these variations; there's still something Chiffchaff about them, since in form and timbre they are reminiscent of syllables in the song. These calls have also been described (cf Siberian Chiffchaff below) as recalling a young chicken (Dean 1985 in Cramp et al.); this emphasises the possibility of confusion with calls from other forms such as *tristis* and *lorenzii*.

Various other calls are heard in courtship and antagonistic situations. The mix of calls in recording C5 was given when 2 birds were in close proximity in early spring; one bird was a male since he had been singing previously, but I was unsure whether the other bird was a male or female, though I suspected female from the manner of the chasing. The calls also seem to correspond to BWP 2b, 5b and 5d, described as excitement song.

Recordings:

1: 56 Song
    1 Northumberland, UK. 7.4.2002 9:30am. 2 sequences – neighbouring males.
    2 Biebrza, Poland. 19.5.2002 1:00pm.
    3 Biebrza, Poland. 29.5.2002 5:00pm.
    4 Northumberland, UK. 4.7.1999 8:45am.
    5 Biebrza, Poland. 29.5.2002 7:00pm. Unusual song.
1: 57 Calls
    1 Northumberland, UK. 7.4.2002 9:30am. Presumed female in territory of one of the birds in S1.
    2 Northumberland, UK. 18.9.2001 10:30am.
    3 Northumberland, UK. 8.9.2002 7:00pm.
    4 Northumberland, UK. 31.8.1997 7:30am. 2 sequences, different birds.
    5 Northumberland, UK. 19.4.1997 7:30am. 2 birds in an encounter and chase.
1: 58 ID

SIBERIAN CHIFFCHAFF
Phylloscopus collybita tristis

There's been a growing interest in Britain over recent years in the small numbers of Siberian Chiffchaffs wintering here. Birds of this form breed from the Pechora basin eastwards and winter mainly in the Indian subcontinent (Cramp et al. 1992). Identification is based on a mixture of difficult plumage features, mainly its cold colourless appearance lacking any green tones, and particularly its call.

The diagnostic call is a rather featureless, whistled 'see', sometimes dropping in pitch slightly at the end; it's been described as like the distress call of a young chicken, a 'lost chick' (Millington 2000) and a high-pitched Bullfinch *Pyrrhula pyrrhula*. Millington describes the song as fast and rather varied, but rarely

heard in Britain.

Scott et al. (1999) discussing the identification of the Mountain Chiffchaff *Phylloscopus lorenzii* describe its call as readily separable from nominate, 'a plain, dry whistle of fairly constant pitch, with the note just falling away at the end', best likened to Bullfinch or Dunnock *Prunella modularis*. This is very close to *tristis*, though they say that *tristis* calls are rather more piercing and even in tone.

Recordings:

1: 59 Song
    R.Ranft/NSA. Northern India.
1: 60 Calls
    P.Holt/NSA. Rajastan, India. 24.2.1997 11:30am.
1: 61 ID

IBERIAN CHIFFCHAFF
Phylloscopus brehmii

Iberian Chiffchaff has a different song and calls from the nominate species, but the song often does not differ as obviously as that of the Siberian birds. Iberian birds' songs lack the very even repetition of syllables of the nominate form and the verse presents a development of variation from first to last; there may be rhythmic changes – a skip in the tempo or a trilled ending (as in Roché 1993). But some songs, as in this recording, could easily pass as an unusual *collybita* Chiffchaff song.

Be aware that nominate birds may give passages at a higher tempo in normal song when excited and song may be irregular after a territorial dispute (Svensson in Cramp et al. 1992).

The calls are clearly different from nominate, a descending 'tsew' (reminiscent of Reed Bunting *Emberiza schoeniclus* calls), compared to nominate's rising 'tweep', though the timbre is similar.

Recordings:

1: 62 Song
    E.Matheu. North-central Spain. May 1997.
1: 63 Calls
    As S1.
1: 64 ID

WILLOW WARBLER *Phylloscopus trochilus*

STATUS: SUMMER VISITOR TO CENTRAL AND NORTHERN EUROPE.
SONG: VERSES OF AN EVENLY PACED, DESCENDING CASCADE OF SLURRED WHISTLES.
SONG SEASON: MAINLY APRIL TO JULY.
CALLS: A WHISTLED, RATHER DISYLLABIC 'HOOEET'.
CONFUSION SPECIES: CHIFFCHAFF, CHAFFINCH (SONG), ODD GREENFINCH PHRASES.

Willow Warblers are one of my favourite singers. It's not that they have an outstanding song or lend themselves to the 'virtuoso' metaphor; it's more that their voice and song pattern are so easy on the ears and their choruses bring a spring warmth to the hillside birch woods of northern Britain.

They are highly territorial when breeding (chases are common) and sometimes in their wintering areas, where song may be heard; some are found in pairs or small groups and foraging with mixed species flocks in late summer and autumn. A small percentage of males in any area tend to be polygynous; yearly figures are 5–17% in Karel'skaya and a maximum of 25% one year in southern England, though some studies in other areas have found polygyny rare. Usually even polygynous males have just a single territory and there's no hostility between 2 females sharing a mate (Cramp et al. 1992).

Males sing from when they arrive on the breeding grounds, beginning around sunrise and continuing through much of the day; in northern Scandinavia at midsummer birds begin singing at night, though there is a quiet period up to around midnight. Birds are heard singing on mornings in the winter areas, though mostly when they first arrive and again towards spring departure (Cramp et al.). Song is also heard on spring migration and while song output wanes from late June through July, birds can be heard singing casually on sunny mornings from late summer into autumn.

At the peak of the breeding season birds tend to sing from favourite song-posts on their territories, a prominent perch at the top or side of a small tree. Otherwise song is often given more casually, pausing from foraging to deliver a verse. Song in flight is rare, other than in antagonistic chases.

A study in Sweden found that the females started to arrive 10–14 days after the males (Radesater et al. 1987). The sequence of pairing correlated well with male song-rate; there was a negative correlation between time spent foraging and song-rate. But another study (Lapshin 1978 in Cramp et al. 1992) suggested that the female's choice of mate is based on his territory rather than the male himself (cf research by Catchpole (1986) on song and territorial correlations with pairing and breeding success in Great Reed Warbler, another partial polygynist).

Song is normally in verses of about 3 seconds, each a cascading sequence of slurred whistles, slightly sibilant, usually descending in pitch through the sequence. Often you can make out distinct phrases of repeated syllables, similar to Chaffinch *Fringilla coelebs*, with which they often share their territories. The first few notes build in volume to a peak, later declining again and slowing slightly towards the end. Though some syllables approach the clipped notes of Chaffinch song and the whistled voice can be quite strident, there are no harsh or percussive elements.

I noticed very little stylistic or tonal difference in the songs of birds I have listened to around Britain and in Poland. I recorded the Polish bird in recording S5, because it sounded a bit different even by the Polish norm, again rather Chaffinch-like in form.

Despite a well-defined song style, there is great variation in the detail of Willow Warbler songs. Research in Germany found that each male has several song-types and those of neighbouring males are usually different; the study also suggested that birds sing longer songs in the late afternoon (Schubert 1967 in Cramp et al.). But it seems that there is variation within song-types, since Cramp et al. also report that in 108 songs of 15 males, only one male sang the same phrase twice.

Unusual songs are occasionally heard from Willow Warblers, including longer more varied versions, songs with trilling or buzzing phrases and Chiffchaff-like phrases (Cramp et al.). Barrett (1948) notes a bird with an extended song, where a normal verse led into a warble, rising and falling sweetly, reminiscent of a Garden Warbler, but always with a Willow Warbler quality. Birds singing a mixed song with Chiffchaff elements are reported to be nearly always Willow Warbler, where identity is established (Cramp et al.);

but there have been instances where Chiffchaff or a hybrid seems likely. The song of *acredula* is thought to be more precisely phrased and at a faster delivery of syllables than nominate, where *yakutensis* (the eastern-most form) has a jerky delivery; but it's not known how typical these characteristics are (Cramp et al.).

The main contact and alarm call of the species is a short whistled 'hooeet', typically with a fuller tone, more drawn-out and disyllabic than the equivalent call of Chiffchaff. The 'hoo' is held for a fraction of a second before rising in pitch more abruptly on the 'eet', where typically the whole Chiffchaff call rises in pitch. In alarm the calls may become sharper and shorter (recording C2), more like Chiffchaff, and variations are heard from juveniles in the autumn.

Excited males often repeat a short, raspy or wheezy note in the intervals between verses of song (BWP 4a, recording C4), homologous to the interstrophic call of Chiffchaff. This call is very similar to the calls of recently fledged young. Other calls are sometimes heard in specific contexts, including a yikkering Cuckoo *Cuculus canorus* alarm call.

The calls of '*yakutensis*-type vagrants' are reported as a sharper 'chweet' in Cramp et al., though the sonograms included represent a brief 'hewit'; it may be that these are easily confused with autumn juveniles (recording C3).

Recordings:
1: 65   Song
    1   Northumberland, UK. 23.4.2000 9:30am.
    2   Northumberland, UK. 27.4.1996 9:30am.
    3   Sutherland, UK. 7.5.1996 8:00am.
    4   Northumberland, UK. 28.4.2002 9:30am.
    5   Biebrza, Poland. 24.5.2002 4:00pm.
    6   SE Finland. 6.6.2002 5:00am.
    7   Northumberland, UK. 22.4.1997 7:00am. An extended verse.
1: 66   Calls
    1   Sutherland, UK. 15.6.1998 4:00pm. 2 adults with recently-fledged young.
    2   Northumberland, UK. 29.6.2001 5:30am.
    3   Northumberland, UK. 25.9.2000 5:00pm. Juvenile autumn.
    4   Northumberland, UK. Males: 3 sequences, April, June & May respectively.
    5   Northumberland, UK. 4.7.1999 9:30am. Juvenile.
    6   All UK. Breeding season.
1: 67   ID

REGULUS

GOLDCREST *Regulus regulus*

STATUS: PARTIAL MIGRANT AND RESIDENT THROUGH MUCH OF EUROPE INTO ASIA.
SONG: VERSES REPEAT A MOTIF TO A CRESCENDO, USUALLY WITH FINAL FLOURISH; HIGH-PITCHED AND SIBILANT.
SONG SEASON: MAINLY MARCH TO JULY.
CALLS: HIGH, THIN WHISTLES, SOME SOFT AND SHORT, SOME LOUD AND LONG; SOME TRILLED.
CONFUSION SPECIES: TREECREEPER (SONG AND CALLS), LONG-TAILED TIT (CALLS), FIRECREST.

Goldcrests usually make their presence known vocally and often they are very vocal birds whether foraging singly, in a pair or in a loose group. All their vocalisations are high-pitched, though subsong often includes some lower-pitched phrases. In human hearing the ageing process affects our perception of higher frequencies first and sadly the voice of the Goldcrest, and presumably Firecrest, usually becomes inaudible in later years.

Their small size means they are very active birds with an almost constant need to be foraging. The mating system is monogamous and though hybridisation with Firecrest has been recorded in captivity, Cramp et al. (1992) only report 2 cases of probable hybridisation in the wild.

Though some groups of birds are resident (e.g. in Britain), there is much movement through dispersal and migration to winter south of breeding range. In winter, small groups (usually 2–7 birds) maintain exclusive territories, which they defend against neighbouring groups, though they may come together to roost (Cramp et al.). In the spring males establish large pre-territories with song and calls, but once paired they maintain smaller nesting territories. Neighbouring males regularly (several times a day) meet at their borders for long 'song-duels' (Haftorn 1986a in Cramp et al.).

Males usually sing while foraging in the foliage at a tree's mid-height, but often lower; occasionally they will fly to the top or some other prominent perch to deliver a few verses in succession. Song is frequent during the breeding season and quite common in February, before breeding, and again in the autumn, particularly a more rambling and warbled subsong which can be as loud as full song.

Birds begin singing before sunrise with a high song-rate (8–11 songs per minute) and, at the start of the breeding season, sing for much of the day, though at a lower song-rate, stopping a little before sunset (Becker 1974b in Cramp et al.). Song-rate and output vary through the breeding stages and are at a minimum during the nestling period.

Song is in verses of around 3 seconds (usually 2.5–4), that build on cycling a rhythmical phrase at a very high pitch, reaching a crescendo usually with a fuller terminal flourish; sometimes the terminal flourish may be omitted, a verse may be run straight into the next and occasionally the cyclical phrase may be extended (exceptionally to over 20 seconds, Cramp et al.). Overall it's a rather stereotyped warble, with a varied ending, in a sweet, slightly sibilant, high-pitched whistle. At peak singing times, intervals between verses are short.

Individual males have a repertoire of endings (minimum 18), some of which are shared with all the males in a local population, others with few; an individual's repertoire remains very constant from year to year (Becker in Cramp et al.). There's geographical variation in the first part of the song as well as in the endings. Birds give a stronger response to local song-types and react very little to very different song-types from other areas.

Song endings often include mimicry, particularly the final note. Recording S2, a kind of loud subsong with much mimicry (included with male song 1a in Cramp et al. and noted as exceptional) features various *Parus* calls, including at least Coal Tit *P. ater*, Chaffinch *Fringilla coelebs* and Long-tailed Tit *Aegithalos caudatus*. A twittering song like the ending of male song is sometimes heard from excited females, particularly associated with male's nest visit.

The calls are mostly high-pitched, sibilant whistles, varying from soft, short contact notes to loud, more sustained and repeated notes, often signifying excitement or intention to fly; birds call readily and the various kinds of call and patterns of calling encompass a functionally complex vocabulary. One parameter of variation in the calls is frequency modulation; the longer calls may be given in a tonally pure form or with fast frequency modulation to sound something like a sibilant trill (and very like Treecreeper *Certhia familiaris*).

It can be very difficult to separate Goldcrest calls from those of Long-tailed Tit or Treecreeper; the short contact calls are also very similar to those of *Parus* species and it's worth noting that all these species readily band together in autumn and winter to forage as a loose flock.

Recordings:

1: 68 Song
  1 Northumberland, UK. 11.7.1999 4:45am.
  2 Northumberland, UK. 9.4.1995 9:00am. 2 sequences.
  3 Northumberland, UK. 14.2.1999 12:15pm.

1: 69 Calls
  1 Northumberland, UK. 1.5.2002 7:00am. 2 sequences.
  2 As S2.
  3 Northumberland, UK. 13.10.1997 6:20pm.

1: 70 ID

FIRECREST *Regulus ignicapillus*

STATUS: SHORT-RANGE MIGRANT IN EUROPE.
SONG: VERSES BUILD TO A CRESCENDO, IN A RHYTHMIC PATTERN ON A SINGLE NOTE; VERY HIGH-PITCHED.
SONG SEASON: APRIL TO JULY, WITH SLIGHT AUTUMN RESUMPTION.

CALLS: VARIOUS HIGH-PITCHED WHISTLES, WITH A PINGING METALLIC RING.
CONFUSION SPECIES: GOLDCREST.

The breeding system is monogamous and territorial and birds tend to be solitary in winter, but will join up with mixed species foraging parties, though details of winter behaviour are few. In cold weather and on migration several will roost together. Like Goldcrests in spring, males set up large territories to begin with, then maintain a much smaller nesting territory (Thaler 1979 in Cramp et al. 1992). In my experience (Britain, France and Spain) Firecrests are generally less vocal birds than Goldcrests, though their actual vocalisations are very similar.

Song-rate is highest before pair formation then declines to a minimum after hatching, with a slight resumption during the fledging period and in autumn. The usual song-rate is between 4 and 7 per minute, depending on stage of breeding, and males begin singing around sunrise – a slightly lower rate and later start than Goldcrest. Subsong is heard from both sexes after breeding and in the autumn (Cramp et al.).

Song is very similar in form to Goldcrest, but lacking a terminal flourish. Where Goldcrest's cyclical phrase has some pitch variation within it, Firecrest's equivalent is little more than a rhythmically repeated note at a constant pitch; and Firecrest's increases the tempo through the sequence, until it runs away with itself at the end, whereas Goldcrest's is at a more or less steady pace, though increasing in power. The overall pitch of the song syllables often drops fractionally during the sequence, where Goldcrest's may rise in pitch, at least up to the terminal flourish.

There is very little audible difference between the songs of the 4 different birds I've recorded in Spain and France, though apparently detailed analysis reveals a more complex structure to these simple-sounding songs. Becker (reported in Cramp et al.), working on individual variation, found that males have a repertoire of song-types (usually 3) which they switch between in bouts of singing. Thaler (also reported in Cramp et al.), studying aviary birds, found that the simplest song-type was used first, at the start of the breeding season, and the structurally most complex type was used by males without a mate.

The main calls are similar high-pitched whistles to Goldcrest including short contact notes 'zit' or 'sisisi', longer drawn-out notes in series and shrill trilling in excitement and courtship. Firecrest's calls tend to be slightly lower-pitched, less sibilant and often with a sharper metallic ring and more percussive voicing than Goldcrest, but this is not an absolute difference. Thaler studied the structure and function of calls of aviary birds in detail and established a complex vocabulary (as Goldcrest), with birds recognising differences in calls very difficult to detect by ear. Both species have a tendency to give the main contact and flight call in groups of 4 (Cramp et al.). A bird I followed for half an hour in Spain foraging through a pine canopy was never heard to call; nor a winter bird I watched in coastal scrub in Northumberland.

Recordings:

1: 71 Song
1   Valencia, Spain. 18.4.2001 2:30pm.
2   Valencia, Spain. 23.4.2001 1:00pm.
3   Languedoc, France. 6.6.1997 8:15pm.

1: 72 Calls
1   K.Turner. Female contact call, while feeding.
2   C.J.Hazevoet. Amsterdam, Netherlands. 21.9.1983 4:30pm.

1: 73 ID

REFERENCES

Baker, K. 1997 *Warblers of Europe, Asia and north Africa.* Christopher Helm

Balsby, T.J.S. 2000 *The function of song in Whitethroats Sylvia communis. Bioacoustics* 11: 17-30

Barrett, J.H. 1948 Unusual song of willow warbler. *Brit. Birds* 41: 150-1

Beckerlegge, J.E. 1951 Winter song of chiffchaff. *Brit. Birds* 44: 94

Bell, D.G. 1960 An encounter with a grasshopper warbler. *Bird Notes* 29: 109-10

Bensch, S. & Hasselquist, D. 1992 Evidence for female choice in a polygynous warbler. *Anim. Behav.* 44: 301-11

Butterfield, D. 2000 Blyth's Reed Warbler in Highland. *Birding World* 13: 277-8

Cade, M. 2000 Sykes's Warbler in Dorset. *Birding World* 13: 274-6

Catchpole, C.K. 1976 Temporal and sequential organisation of song in the sedge warbler (*Acrocephalus schoenobaenus*). *Behaviour* 59: 226-47

Catchpole, C.K. 1980 Sexual selection and the evolution of complex songs among warblers of the genus *Acrocephalus. Behaviour* 74: 149-66

Catchpole, C.K. 1983 Variation in the song of the great reed warbler *Acrocephalus arundinaceus* in relation to mate attraction and territorial defence. *Anim. Behav.* 31: 1217-25

Catchpole, C.K. 1986 Song repertoires and reproductive success in the great reed warbler *Acrocephalus arundinaceus. Behav. Ecol. Sociobiol.* 19: 439-45

Catchpole, C.K. & Leisler, B. 1989 Variation in the song of the aquatic warbler *Acrocephalus paludicola* in response to playback of different song structures. *Behaviour* 108: 125-38

Catchpole, C.K. & Slater, P.J.B. 1995 *Bird Song. Biological themes and variations.* Cambridge University Press

Cramp, S. (ed) 1992 *The Birds of the Western Palearctic.* Vol VI. Oxford University Press

Curber, R.M. 1969 Blackcap imitating song of lesser spotted woodpecker. *Brit. Birds* 62: 543-4

Dowsett-Lemaire, F. 1979a The imitative range of the song of the marsh warbler *Acrocephalus palustris*, with special reference to imitations of African birds. *Ibis* 121: 453-68

Dowsett-Lemaire, F. 1979b Vocal behaviour of the Marsh Warbler *Acrocephalus palustris. Gerfault* 69: 475-502

Harrap, S. 1989 The difficulties of Reed, Marsh and Blyth's Reed Warbler identification. *Birding World* 2: 318-24

Hinde, R.A. & Thom, A.S. 1947 The breeding of the moustached warbler in Cambridgeshire. *Brit. Birds* 40: 98-104

Hoffman, H.J. 1949 Probable singing by female grasshopper warbler. *Brit. Birds* 42: 58-9

Ireland, D.T. 1984 Nocturnal singing by Cetti's warblers. *Brit. Birds* 77: 212

Kettle, R. & Ranft, R. 1992 *British Bird Sounds on CD.* British Library

King, J. 1998 Lesser Whitethroat taxonomy. *Birding World* 1: 122

Klit, I. 1999 The function of song forms in the Lesser Whitethroat *Sylvia curruca. Bioacoustics* 10: 31-45

Koskimies, P. 1980 Breeding biology of Blyth's Reed Warbler *Acrocephalus dumetorum* in SE Finland. *Ornis Fennica* 57: 26-32

Lemaire, F. 1977 Mixed song, interspecific competition and hybridisation in the Reed and Marsh Warblers (*Acrocephalus scirpaceus* and *Acrocephalus palustris*). *Behaviour* 63: 215-40

Madge, S.C. 1990 Separating Radde's and Dusky Warblers. *Birding World* 3: 281-5

Madge, S.C. 1992 Identification of Moustached Warbler. *Birding World* 5: 299-303

May, D.J. & Manning, A. 1951 The breeding cycle of a pair of wood warblers. *Brit. Birds* 44: 5-10

McGregor, P.K. 1988 Song length and 'male quality' in the chiffchaff. *Anim. Behav.* 36: 606-8

Millington, R. 1998 *Locustella* warblers in autumn 1998. *Birding World* 11: 387-9

Millington, R. 2000 Siberian Chiffchaffs in Worcestershire. *Birding World* 13: 58-9

Millington, R. & Mullarney, K. 2000 Hume's Yellow-browed Warbler identification. *Birding World* 13: 447

Money, D. 2000 Desert Lesser Whitethroat on Teesside. *Birding World* 13: 451-3

Mullarney, K. et al. 1999 *Collins Bird Guide.* HarperCollins

Page, D. 1999 Identification of Bonelli's Warblers. *Brit. Birds* 92: 524

Paull, D.E. 1977 Do blackcaps have a wryneck call? *Brit. Birds* 70: 458

Pearson, D.J., Small, B.J., & Kennerley, P.R. 2002 Eurasian Reed Warbler: the characters and variation associated with the Asian form *fuscus. Brit. Birds* 95: 42

Pettersen, M. 2001 A Central Asian Lesser Whitethroat in Sweden. *Birding World* 14: 12-15

Radesater, T. et al. 1987 Song rate and pair formation in the willow warbler *Phylloscopus trochilus. Anim. Behav.* 35: 1645-51

Roché, J.C. 1993 *All the bird songs of Britain and Europe on 4 CDs.* Sittelle

Scott, M., Siddle, J. & Shirihai, H. 1999 Mountain Chiffchaff. *Birding World* 12: 163-7

Shirihai, H. et al. 1995 Identification and taxonomy of large *Acrocephalus* warblers. *Dutch Birding* 17: 229-39

Shirihai, H., Gargallo, G. & Helbig, A.J. 2001 *Sylvia Warblers. Identification, taxonomy and phylogeny of the genus Sylvia.* Christopher Helm

Simms, E. 1985 *British Warblers.* Collins

Svensson, L. 2001 Identification of Eastern and Western Olivaceous, Booted and Sykes's Warblers. *Birding World* 14: 192-219

Svensson, L. 2002 Split personalities. *Birdwatch* 119: May 2002

Taylor, R. 1994 *Butlleti del Parc Natural de s'Albufera de Mallorca.* Vol. 1

Temrin, H. 1986 Singing behaviour in relation to polyterritorial polygyny in the wood warbler (*Phylloscopus sibilatrix*). *Anim. Behav.* 34: 146-52

Vinicombe, K. 2000 Siberian exiles – identification. *Birdwatch* 102: December 2000

Vinicombe, K. 2002 A tale of two warblers. *Birdwatch* 118: April 2002

Wilson, T.J. & Fentiman, C. 1999 Eastern Bonelli's Warbler in Scilly: new to Britain and Ireland. *Brit. Birds* 92: 1